WILDLIFE

OF ATLANTIC CANADA & NEW ENGLAND

PHOTOGRAPHY BY WAYNE BARRETT · TEXT BY GARY SAUNDERS

DEDICATION

To the children of today and tommorrow

ACKNOWLEDGEMENTS

Growing up in Newfoundland's Notre Dame Bay in the 1940s, I lived in a wildlife paradise and didn't know it. It was this, and my father's almost inordinate love for things wild, that shaped my first responses to wildlife.

Later, as a young forester, I was privileged to travel the wilds with expert naturalists like Hans Mandoe, Tom Dammond and Neil Van Nostrand. They were my local counterparts of literary mentors like Thoreau, Aldo Leopold and Victor Cahalane.

Writing the text to accompany Wayne Barrett's evocative wildlife photographs was like revisiting those haunts and reviving those friendships.

Among my written sources for this book I owe a particular debt to Richard M. De Graaf's and Deborah D. Rudis's comprehensive *New England Wildlife: Habitat, Natural History, and Distribution.*

And I thank Ross Baker for his comments on the Land Birds section. Any errors that remain, there or elsewhere in the text, are my own.

Gary L. Saunders

I wish to express my gratitude to Noel O'Dea and Darlene Marshall of Marine Adventure Tours, Paul Lannon of Air Nova, Birt Visser of Shubenacadie Wildlife Park, the Staff of PEI Parks, and to Alanna Sobey for her support and photographic assistance. A special thanks to my wife, Anne MacKay, and our daughters, Laura and Amy.

Wayne Barrett

Nimbus Publishing Limited
P.O. Box 9301, Station A
Halifax, Nova Scotia
B3K 5N5

Design by Steven Slipp, GDA, Halifax
Printed and bound in Hong Kong by Everbest Printing Company, Ltd.

All photographs taken by Wayne Barrett except for the following which were provided by Ted Levin: pages iv c-b, 5, 26, 27, 33 72, 94, 98, 102

Canadian Cataloguing in Publication Data
Saunders, Gary L.
Wildlife of Atlantic Canada and New England
ISBN 1-55109-0080-2
1. Zoology—Atlantic Provinces. 2. Zoology—New England.
I. Barrett, Wayne. II. Title.

QL151.S38 1992 591.97 C92-098512-2

CONTENTS

INTRODUCTION v

MAMMALS vi

LAND MAMMALS...3
  Plant-Eaters 4
  Meat-Eaters 16
  Insect-Eaters 26
  Omnivores 28

SEA MAMMALS 34
  Seals 36
  Toothed Whales 39
  Baleen Whales 40

BIRDS 44

LAND BIRDS 46

PERCHING BIRDS 56

OTHER BIRDS 65

SHOREBIRDS AND ALLIES...69

WATER BIRDS 73

AMPHIBIANS & REPTILES 90

AMPHIBIANS 91
  Salamanders 91
  Frogs and Toads 93

REPTILES 98
  Freshwater Turtles...98
  Saltwater Turtles 100
  Snakes...103

INTRODUCTION

Facing page, far left: Muy Coyote in Spanish means very cunning. This smaller cousin of the Wolf arrived in the Northeast only in the last few decades. Originally a dweller of western prairie and scrubland, it has adapted well to our farm and woodlot habitat and is here to stay.

Facing page, centre top: Although Whales routinely flash their flukes on sounding (diving), lobtailing differs in that the animal stands on its head and holds its flukes aloft for some moments before going under.

Facing page, centre bottom: The little Northern Red-bellied Snake has a bewildering array of brownish colour phases and patterns, but the underside of the body is always orange, bordered by a dark mottled strip.

Facing page, near left: The ideal habitat for the Bald Eagle consists of a shallow, ice-free inlet abounding in coarse fish such as flounder, sculpin, and eel, with a tall tree for nesting. The white or "bald" head is a mark of sexual maturity usually attained in the fourth year.

THROUGHOUT THE NORTHEAST, ON FARMS AND feedlots, in homes and pet shops, we see domesticated animals. Glossy riding horses and placid dairy cattle graze in summer pastures or munch in snug winter barns. In long, low, aluminum buildings eggs from twenty thousand hens roll down chutes to be graded, washed, and packed for market. Inside our homes, pet cats, dogs, budgies, and even reptiles occupy us. All these domesticated creatures must be fed, housed, and cared for virtually every day of their lives.

Beyond the safety and comfort of our towns and farms, however, millions of other creatures feed and care for themselves. They range from tiny newts foraging under forest leaf mould to mighty humpback whales ploughing through Atlantic swells. Because they live wild, without help from us, they are called wildlife. We admire them, study them, try to get close to them. Why?

The more that urbanization squeezes nature from our everyday experience, the more we seem to look to nature for solace and guidance. Thousands of us keep backyard bird feeders. Thousands clutch binoculars and cameras and go hiking, bird-watching, whale-watching. More than two hundred thousand Atlantic Canadians hunt, fish, and trap; many do so as much to experience the woods and lakes and marshes as to kill anything. In unprecedented numbers we visit zoos and wildlife parks, watch television shows on wildlife and our environment, and buy books on natural history. We are worried. With poet Gerard Manley Hopkins, we cry:

> What would the world be, once bereft
> Of wet and of wilderness? Let them be left,
> O let them be left, wildness and wet;
> Long live the weeds and the wilderness yet.

And yet, as much as we profess to admire wildness it frightens us. After all, what would happen to our cherished lifestyles if we took people like Hopkins and Henry David Thoreau at their word? How could we reconcile our spendthrift use of natural resources with such a philosophy?

This is largely what the environmental debate is about. Whatever its outcome, we need not fear wildness. In extolling its virtues, people like Hopkins and Thoreau were not commending Darwin's survival of the fittest as a guide for human affairs— though some prefer to believe that. No, they were exhorting us to get in touch with wildness, to restore our lost connection to the ancient rhythms of sun and moon, plants and tide; the rhythms which govern wild things.

Despite our long history of human settlement, we are still rich in wildlife. Our diverse geology, topography, climate, and history have created unique flora and fauna. Not only in wilderness areas, but throughout the region, wildlife continues to look after itself. Our task, besides striving to undo the harm we have done, is to hinder wildlife as little as humanly possible and to help it where we can. For we are all in this together.

—Gary Lloyd Saunders
Old Barns, Nova Scotia
October 1991

MAMMALS

OF ALL EARTH'S TEAMING CREATURES, ONLY ONE group feeds its babies with mother's milk. Members of this group are called mammals because the milk is produced by special glands called *mammae*. From the same Latin root we get "Mama" and "Mom."

More than 200 million years ago when the continents tore apart to form the Atlantic Ocean, the first furry mammals were already hunting insects at night to escape the terrible lizards that ruled the day.

Although small and defenceless, they had exquisitely tuned senses of touch, hearing, and smell. These were linked to comparatively large brains able to store and process images and information in new ways. A new kind of intelligence was abroad. In time, they could outrun any lizard and swim and fly as well as any fish or bird. But most importantly, instead of laying fragile shelled eggs with a built-in food supply as did fish, amphibians, reptiles, and birds, mammals began to nurture their young safely inside their bodies. Some, like today's kangaroo, arranged for the embryo to complete most of its development in a warm outside pocket. Others nourished their young for the full term off the mother's bloodstream by a special filter called the placenta. Afterward they ensured a high survival rate by suckling, guarding, and coaching them until they could live on their own.

Some 60 million years ago, when the Appalachians had worn down like old teeth and the Rockies were new, the dinosaurs were gone. Land mammals were spreading everywhere, and a few even ventured back into the ocean. Whales and seals are believed to be land mammals that long ago returned to the sea. Seals still breed on land or floating ice; whales have left it for good, though they sometimes come close to feed, raise young, or scrape off barnacles and sea lice.

A few million years ago when the first campfires glimmered in the African night, other mammals—great elephants, apes and wild horses, tiny monkeys and shrews, the wild cats and dogs, seals and great whales—were all on stage.

Then came the latest global refrigeration. By forcing us to perfect the use of fire and tools, the ice ages transformed a weak and almost naked mammal into earth's most powerful creature. Yet without the Woolly Mammoth, Reindeer, and wild Ox, we could not have survived that ordeal. Their bodies clothed and fed us; their spirits nurtured our first inklings of religion and art. We needed them more than they did us. By the time stone age hunter-gatherers wandered into what is now Atlantic Canada and New England some ten thousand years ago, this relationship was already ancient. For eons the ancestors of today's Algonquian and Inuit peoples hunted caribou and seal beneath the ice-mantled hills. Then, as the warming climate cleared the seas of summer ice, forests of maple, oak, and pine replaced larch, willow, and birch. Southern species like Black Bear, Moose, and Bobcat followed, and the range of the marine mammals shifted northward.

The warm-blooded mammals adapted to every available niche or living space on sea and land, from ocean shallows and deeps to marshes, caves, treetops, and even the air.

When the first Europeans settled the region in the mid-1600s, the fauna was much like it is today. The mammals consisted of some seventy species, fifty of them terrestrial. The twenty species of sea mammals frequented the harbours and oceans in far greater numbers than today. One of these, the Walrus or "Sea-Cow," was com-

Facing page: *A mother Porcupine and her baby born after a gestation of some two hundred days. The baby's quills are fully operational within hours. A measure of the success of this armour is the Porcupine's ability to maintain its population with only one offspring per mature female a year. Porcupines live for about six years in the wild.*

Facing page: *While Black Bears are generally harmless, mothers with cubs should be given a wide berth. This mother Black Bear foraging with her cub is an example of the cinnamon phase. Born in a snug den sometime in February, this cub nursed from its sleeping mother until warm weather roused her. They will fatten on everything from greens to ants to dead meat until late fall. Then they will hibernate together.*

mon off the Gulf of St. Lawrence coast of New Brunswick. Unfortunately, French settlers killed them for their oil and ivory, and by the late 1700s they had vanished.

The teeming populations of whale and seal did not escape the impact of the newcomers either. Whale oil was popular in Europe as an all-purpose lubricant, a primary source of light, and an additive in products ranging from drugs to soap to pitch. As Old World stocks declined, the Europeans turned to new sources. A fifty-five gallon barrel of oil from the "New Founde Lande" was worth the equivalent of more than five thousand dollars.

By the 1570s as many as nine hundred Basque sailors summered at Red Bay in Labrador, taking an enormous toll on native species, including the now extinct Atlantic Gray Whale. After the Spanish lost their foothold, there was a lull in commercial whaling until the New Englanders and Scandinavians revived and expanded it. Vastly increased commercial fishing of surface species, like herring and caplin, also took its toll by reducing the food supply.

Seals were killed for their fat and fur. Settlers first hunted them with gaffs or guns either on foot or from small boats. Then the Newfoundlanders introduced "seal fishing": hemp nets were strung between headlands and islands and raised or lowered by winches. These nets intercepted the seals as they swam south on their midwinter migration.

By the 1860s steam-powered vessels met the main herds far offshore and the slaughter for oils and fur began in earnest.

LAND MAMMALS

THE ORIGINAL ALGONQUIAN AND INUIT PEOPLES lived for millennia in harmony with their environment. With the arrival of the Europeans, this changed. Fur, hides, meat, and oil suddenly became commercial commodities and European technology began to replace Native ways.

Moreover, land use and abuse altered the habitat. While the Natives had burned the woods regularly to improve hunting, their impact was minor compared with the land clearing, logging, and increased forest fires that followed settlement. Conflagrations like New Brunswick's huge Miramichi Fire of 1825 created sunlit openings and barrens of unprecedented size. This tipped the balance away from the flora and fauna of the dim, moist, climax forest toward the light-loving pioneer plants and animals that go with warm sunny clearings.

By the 1920s these forces, perhaps abetted by climatic change, had killed off Woodland Caribou in New Brunswick and Nova Scotia and brought our two largest carnivores, the Eastern Cougar and Gray Wolf, to extinction here. Meanwhile uncontrolled trapping decimated the Beaver, extirpated the Giant Sea Mink and Wolverine, and very nearly wiped out the Marten and Fisher.

Disease also played a part in the distribution of wildlife. An example is the severe outbreak of distemper in the 1920s and 1930s that killed off the Skunk in Nova Scotia. Even today skunks are still absent from Nova Scotia's western counties.

Of the surviving land mammals, not all occupy the entire region. For instance, the island of Newfoundland lacks more than a dozen Maritime species whose northeastward migration after the ice ages was blocked by the rising ocean. The fauna of Cape Breton Island and Prince Edward Island show similar gaps: Porcupine are missing from both and the latter has no Moose, White-tailed Deer, Lynx, or Bobcat.

On the other hand, Newfoundland has interesting examples of wildlife that might never have arrived had they not been deliberately introduced. Around 1870 concern over winter meat shortages in the outports prompted the government to introduce Snowshoe Hare from the Maritimes. These prolific newcomers soon put fresh meat on outport tables.

Newfoundland also successfully introduced Maritime Moose in 1878 to the Gander River and 1904 to the Howley area, and in the 1970s brought in Red Squirrel, Chipmunk, and Shrew—the latter to control Larch Sawfly. Meanwhile, escaped ranch Mink established themselves and wrought havoc with the Island's wild Muskrat.

Human activity has played a role in the movement of many species to new territory. The Coyote is a recent wildlife phenomenon in all four provinces. The original habitat of this intelligent wild dog was the west. However, as land was cleared and rail and road building spread, the Coyote moved to the east and north.

Consider as well the Bobcat's arrival on Cape Breton Island. Until the Canso Causeway was opened in 1955, the Bobcat was unknown to Cape Breton. The Lynx had the run of the island, stalking Snowshoe Hare and other prey. However, the opening of the causeway provided access to new lowland hunting grounds for the Bobcat. The Lynx, better adapted to deep snow, retreated to the uplands. Today in Atlantic Canada and New England, we have some two dozen species of plant-eaters (herbivores), a dozen meat-eaters (carnivores), four that eat a smorgasbord of animal and plant food (omnivores), and some nineteen species of insect-eaters.

All our land mammals can swim if need be, but very few make it a habit, and even fewer take to salt water. Only one group, the Bat, has mastered true flight.

Unlike their marine cousins, land mammals need no heavy coat of blubber to ward off the constant ocean chill and create buoyancy. However, they do have to cope with heat. To maintain even temperatures in the heat of summer, they shed their winter coats, seek shade, pant, and loll in cool water. In preparation for winter, they put on fat and replace their summer coats with ones that also have a waterproof outer shell but a much thicker undercoat of dense, air-trapping fur.

In some ways land mammals have it tougher than other animals. Migrating birds escape the worst of our winters. Cold-blooded amphibians and reptiles sleep the winter away in the earth or under a lake bottom. However, most of our resident mammals must be out in all weathers, finding food, shelter, and safety.

PLANT-EATERS

The chief advantage for the herbivore is that there is nearly always something to eat. The disadvantages are that plant food is low in energy and a lot of time must be spent foraging.

Each group of herbivore has its own strategies for getting food, conserving energy, and evading predators. Most are fleet footed, some can jump, and some are agile tree climbers. A few are at home in the water. Some are miners, and one is an accomplished civil engineer. One of the species repels predators with a swish of its tail. Another changes colour to match its environment. Yet another emits a foul odour and feigns death.

These and other skills are tested to the utmost in winter, when greens and fruit are scarce and roots are frozen in the earth. One group has this problem solved. Their chisel-shaped teeth allow them to gnaw through the husks of stored nuts and seeds. Others are adept at cropping the woody stems and buds of perennial plants for the nourishment inside.

Although most plant-eaters hole up in bitter weather, one relies on total hibernation. Many resort to hidden nests with ample larders. Two aquatic species retire to well-stocked, moated fortresses.

Atlantic Canada's wild land herbivores of today are represented by Caribou, Moose, White-tailed Deer, Arctic and Snowshoe Hare, Woodchuck or Groundhog, Porcupine, three types of Squirrel, one Chipmunk, and seven species of Mouse. Beaver and Muskrat occupy mainly wetland habitats. New England has the same fauna, enriched by two species of Cottontail Rabbit, the Gray Fox, the Southern Flying Squirrel, two more Shrews, a Mole, and two more Mice. It also boasts the region's only marsupial (pouch) mammal, the Virginia Opossum.

Mice are high on every predator's menu. In other words they are at the very bottom of the predator food chain. Even reptiles and frogs catch them. Against this relentless onslaught their only weapon is relentless reproduction. Besides eating their own weight every twenty-four hours, this is their chief end in life. Among our several woodland and meadow species—including two species of dainty White-Footed or Deer Mice and two long-tailed Jumping Mice— the one that bears

the brunt of this onslaught is the humble Meadow Vole. Short-tailed, low-slung, and plump it races about in search of seeds and greens to maintain its frantic pace of up to seventeen litters a year. An eighteen-month-old Meadow Mouse is ancient and doddering.

The House Mouse and Norway Rat, imported to Atlantic Canada and New England in the holds of ships, are almost as busy. Daily, they consume and waste food equal to two-thirds their own weight. Usually, this is at the expense of humans, as these destructive mammals gnaw through wood, plaster, and electrical wiring. These rodents are frequently used for medical research.

Above: *Life is risky for all wild mice because so many predators hunt them day and night. A White-footed or Deer Mouse crouches until the coast is clear. White underparts and immaculate grooming distinguish it from the all gray, often unkempt, House Mouse.*

Facing page: *Slightly larger than the Red Squirrel, this dark-phase Gray Squirrel pauses on a maple branch to eye the photographer. Gray Squirrels are common throughout New England except in northern Maine, and range west to southern Manitoba and south to Texas and Florida.*

Right: *Mainly a ground dweller, the Chipmunk depends heavily on camouflage to escape hawks and other predators as it hunts for fallen nuts and seeds near its den.*

Above: *Although chiefly a tree dweller, the Red or Fox Squirrel often descends to feed—especially if someone tosses it a peanut. It readily comes to human dwellings and in winter frequents bird feeders looking for easy food.*

Like the wild mice, Squirrels and Chipmunks also favour nuts and seeds. In Atlantic Canada and northern New England, three kinds of Squirrel and one Chipmunk species enliven the woods and parks.

The Red or Fox Squirrel is surely one of the best loved of all land mammals. When disturbed it chatters and scolds noisily to the delight of hikers and the disgust of hunters. Against cold or rainy weather it maintains a snug treetop penthouse, where in early spring three to seven young are born.

Somewhat larger, the Gray Squirrel shares a mixed woods habitat of beech, oak, pine, spruce, and fir. Both squirrels regularly cache seeds and nuts, but neither finds them by memory; they do it by smell. Often missed seeds germinate to generate a food supply for future squirrels.

It's a pity so few of us ever see the nocturnal Flying Squirrel. This captivating little creature hides by day in a den, usually the renovated nest cavity of a Downy Woodpecker. Its large bulging eyes give good night vision, while loose skin flaps between the front and back paws equip it for gliding. Launching from treetop height, Flying Squirrels have been known to swoop fifty metres—more on steep slopes. They usually land low in a tree, streak to the top, and again launch

Above: *Paddling with webbed feet and steering with its flat scaly tail, a beaver hurries about its work. When submerged its ears and nostrils are closed. To keep from drowning while chewing, the animal seals its lips behind the front teeth. Moments after this picture was taken the Beaver slapped its tail on the water as a warning and dived.*

Facing page: *Like the Beaver, Muskrats feed on a variety of aquatic vegetation. This one is eating a fresh blade of cattail it has cut. Since Muskrats do not store food, they must forage under and over the ice all winter.*

into space. Or they may race across the undulating canopy from treetop to treetop. No North American mammal is more agile. Like its larger relatives, it sometimes kills and eats small birds and devours small birds' eggs.

Everyone loves the Eastern Chipmunk, a sort of scaled-down Red Squirrel with racing stripes. Found throughout the Northeast but never plentifully, it requires mixed-wood slopes with plenty of brush and rocks to hide under and loose soil for burrowing. Its mainstay is nuts and seeds supplemented by berries, insects, and mushrooms. In spring, it chews the bark of maple trees and laps up the oozing sap.

Beaver and Muskrat have both mastered their semi-aquatic habitats; but there the resemblance ends. Compared with the Beaver, the Muskrat has a very limited engineering repertoire. All it can manage is a pushup, a dome of reeds and rushes. Beavers, on the other hand, think nothing of damming a large stream in several places, constructing a timbered and plastered lodge big enough to hold a family of five or six, and digging a system of canals to help them bring home the many trees they must fell for construction and food.

Beaver impoundments—often several on one stream—make rich habitat for fish, waterfowl, mink, and otter. When the beavers abandon the stream to look for an area with more trees, the dams let go and ready-made "beaver meadows" are created. These provided farming opportunities for the first settlers.

It was not for such feats that Canada chose this animal as its national symbol, however. The Beaver got that honour for its role in the fur trade that opened up the country.

Muskrats like their wetlands ready-made. Their habitat are wide marshlands with plenty of cattails for food and shelter and slow winding streams that offer muddy banks overhung with alder and willow. Muskrats dine mainly on water vegetation, but telltale shell heaps reveal a taste for an occasional snack of freshwater clams.

In spite of being heavily trapped since colonial times, this fertile rodent is in no danger of extinction so long as suitable streams and wetlands exist. Each mature female produces one to three litters of four to nine young a year. Thoreau, talking about the value of wildness, once spoke symbolically of killing and eating a "musquash." Actually the meat is tasty and sweet. In the 1920s, chic New York restaurants sold it as "Marsh Hare."

Despite all the trapping and heavy predation by Mink and other carnivores, the Muskrat can be quite nonchalant. Writer Annie Dillard tells of seeing a very much alive young muskrat drifting lazily downstream on its back, eyes closed, front paws folded demurely on its chest.

Equipped with superb hearing and powerful hind legs, our two species of hare are the region's fleetest ground mammals. If pursued the Snowshoe Hare or "Rabbit" bounds away, clearing three-metre ravines with ease, hopping high to check on the enemy's progress, and making sudden ninety-degree turns to throw it off course. In summer its brown and white fur blends with the forest floor; in winter a white coat helps it fade into the snowy landscape.

During the warmer months hares eat leaves and grasses. In winter they turn to the twigs and bark of aspen, maple, willow, and brambles, adding some evergreens for spice.

In mid-May the female gives birth in a sheltered nest to her first litter of two to nine. The young are born fully furred and with their eyes

Facing page: *Scratching one's ear with a snowshoe can be awkward. But in deep fluffy snow the Snowshoe Hare's fully oversized hind foot buoys its body up, allowing it to leave a bobcat floundering far behind. By the first snowfall the Hare's summer coat—all but the black ear tips—will be turning white.*

wide open. Within days they start adding greens to their milk diet. Around mid-June the mother weans them to make room for family number two. In late July a third litter appears.

This legendary fertility offsets the heavy natural predation to which this animal is subject. The Hare's habit of following well-worn paths makes it easy to snare. Hunters and trappers routinely take more than a million each year in Atlantic Canada for the delicious meat. The chief causes of mortality, however, are disease and stress, which regularly decimate hare populations over wide areas in ten-year cycles.

Hereabouts the Arctic Hare, though still common in the Canadian Arctic and Greenland, is found naturally only in Labrador and in remote uplands like Newfoundland's Buchans Plateau. To protect the species, Newfoundland has set up isolated populations in places like Brunette Island in Fortune Bay.

Preferring rocky hillsides and low mountains, this hare is two to three times as heavy as its woodland counterpart. Although shy in summer, in winter it seems almost tame. Willow is its standard year-round fare, supplemented by crowberry and other alpine plants in summer. These hares are fond of sunbathing, but when they venture to the shore it is to feed on kelp. When attacked by a fox or lynx on flat ground they dodge with lightning speed, but sometimes they miscalculate. In hilly terrain they scoot straight up the cliffs and soon leave the pursuer behind. Females bear one litter of five to seven young a year.

The Eastern Cottontail (*Sylvilagus*) is like a Varying Hare with smaller hind feet and thinner fur. It occupies most of eastern North America south of Canada including the southern half of New England and prefers fields and forest edges.

Cottontails do not turn white in winter.

In western Connecticut there are also small numbers of the European Hare (*Lepus capensis*). Introduced from Europe to New York between 1890 and 1910, enough have escaped to form small colonies here and there in open country.

The Porcupine never hurries; it doesn't need to. A porcupine's quills can kill. Ranging from one to six centimetres long, each whitish hollow shaft is tipped with many very sharp, tiny, black barbs. When an enemy bites a porcupine the quills come loose and stick in its face and throat. A good swipe from the mammal's powerful tail can embed hundreds. As the victim moves, they work their way into its muscles and organs, often causing death by infection and internal injury. It takes a strong pull with pliers to remove them from a dog's nose and mouth.

With such formidable weaponry this animal, which weighs about fourteen kilograms, has little to fear. Fishers and Bobcats kill some, however motor vehicles account for most deaths.

The porcupine's bearlike claws enable it to climb slowly to where it last dined. In winter this might be the upper bark of a tamarack, pine, or spruce. Since girdled trees die about the wound, this angers woodlot owners and foresters. If, as is common, a family shares one den, most of the evergreens within thirty metres may be peeled and dying. In summer it is fond of aspen leaves, and may graze on clover in a nearby field.

Mating occurs in late fall, preceded by odd vocalizations including grunts, moans, and screams. It is a risky business. During copulation the female lays her quills either flat or loose with her tail to one side. In May or June one baby is born, still sheathed in its amniotic sac. Within minutes the hefty youngster can use its tiny quills,

Facing page: *A prime White-tail buck in autumn, its antlers free of velvet, ignores biting flies as it listens for a faint rustle that may signal danger or a potential mate.*

Below: *This White-tail fawn was born in late May after a two-hundred-day gestation. By mid-summer it has lost most of its natal spots.*

and by the second day it can climb trees.

Looking like a small porcupine without quills, the Groundhog or Woodchuck relies for safety on its skill as a miner. It can climb if necessary, but prefers to burrow under tree roots, woodpiles, or among rocks. These tunnels may extend a dozen metres or more with several entrances for security. Normally, they are below frost level. This is where the animal lives from September through late winter. Until then it fattens on clover, grasses, flowers, thistles, garden vegetables, and farm crops. They especially like wild fruit.

Once asleep the animal barely breathes, its pulse weakens, and the body grows cold. During hibernation the body burns off two or three centimetres of white fat built up over the summer. So profound is its slumber that if brought into a warm room the Groundhog cannot wake for several hours. The belief that groundhogs emerge on the second day of February and go back for another six weeks' sleep if they see their shadows is delightful, but pure legend.

Atlantic Canada is home to three members of the deer family, namely White-tailed Deer (*Odocoileus*), Moose (*Alces*), and Woodland Caribou (*Rangifer*). Caribou, being reindeer, favour a subarctic existence, but Deer prefer temperate forest. This partly accounts for the postglacial disappearance of Caribou from all but Newfoundland and Labrador and the influx of White-tails as the climate warmed. Moose are an intermediate species.

All three have cloven hooves and chew the cud like domestic cattle. Unlike cattle the males grow temporary horns or antlers each year. Nourished all summer by a blood-rich velvety coating, these grow rapidly. As the leaves turn colour, the animals rub their antlers against trees and rocks, removing the velvet and exposing the rich mahogany weapons. These are soon used to establish harems and defend territory. By first snow the antlers are mostly shed. Few are ever found because mice and porcupines consume them for the minerals they contain. Female Caribou commonly have antlers; female Moose and Deer do not.

In the 1940s, when deer populations peaked, Moose commonly appeared in towns and villages, acting strangely. It was discovered that these animals had been infected by a parasitic brain worm carried by White-tails. While harmless to the White-tails, it was often lethal to Moose and

Facing page: *Weighing up to 635 kilograms, a mature bull Moose stands more than two metres at the shoulder. Although it can gore and lift a smaller rival clear off the ground, most disputes between males during the September-October rut or mating season are settled without bloodshed.*

Below: *A Woodland Caribou stag and its harem graze in bog and barren habitat. They are part of Newfoundland's Avalon Peninsula herd, an offshoot of the main herd that populates the interior south and west of Gander and Red Indian lakes.*

Caribou. Fortunately White-tails prefer domesticated woodlots and farmland, while Moose seek wilder landscapes. The failure of recent attempts to re-introduce Woodland Caribou into Cape Breton Island and Maine may be due in part to this parasite.

Moose are often pictured belly-deep in water with water lilies dangling from their huge dripping mouths. Dining in shallow lakes is indeed one of their favourite summer pastimes. By completely submerging now and then, they also escape the biting flies that plague all warm-blooded creatures in summer.

In the autumn they face a more serious threat,

the hunter. Skilled guides call curious bulls to within shooting range by imitating the mating moan of a cow moose.

In winter Moose generally seek frozen swamps or recently burnt or harvested land looking for thickets of balsam fir and birch to eat. During severe weather, White-tails and Moose share the trait of holing up in hardwood yards. These areas are sheltered by thick evergreens and provide food. One deer needs a large armful of browse each day to survive. When all the cedar, birch, and maple twigs within reach are consumed, many deer will starve rather than leave the yard's walkways to flounder in shoulder-high snow in search of more food. The longer-legged and stronger moose are better able to survive such conditions.

Woodland Caribou are not long-legged but their hooves serve as built-in shovels. As winter snows deepen in the spruce bogs and river bottoms where Caribou foraged on greens and tree lichens all summer, they venture onto upland barrens where wind sweeps the ground bare. When necessary they dig through crusted snow with their broad and sharp-edged hooves to reach the lichens and green plants below.

Caribou are more communal and migratory than Deer or Moose. In Newfoundland, before lumber camps depleted the interior herds in the early 1900s, passenger trains had to wait for days while Caribou crossed the track. For centuries Beothuk hunters had intercepted such herds at selected river crossings with long, deer fences made of half-cut trees.

Today's Woodland Caribou still migrate in small herds from winter to summer range, their hooves clicking as of old. Rivers and lakes pose no problem. With their hollow outer hair and large

Above: *This Caribou grazes undisturbed on lichens and greens.*

Facing page: *Almost extinct in the Northeast since the 1800s, the magnificent Gray Wolf now survives here only in places like Nova Scotia's Provincial Wildlife Park. Its principal prey, the Caribou, was decimated on the mainland by forest fires, logging, overhunting, and perhaps climatic warming.*

hooves, Caribou are buoyant, strong swimmers. Pregnant does journey a few days ahead, give birth in a sheltered valley, and then rejoin the herd. Newborn calves can easily keep up.

MEAT-EATERS

Like the human family with whom it has fraternized for some four thousand years, the dog family (*Canidae*) excels at socializing and long-distance running. The Wolf, the Coyote, and even the family pet, if allowed to roam the woods, are similar in behaviour. By nature they scent, track, and run down prey as a cooperative venture. After a successful hunt, each participant gets a share according to rank and seniority. They love family gatherings with lots of barking, singing, and roughhousing. Only the Red Fox tends to be a loner.

The dog tribe communicates by an array of voice, scent, and body language. Howling, territorial urinating, and tail-wagging are among the better known expressions. Their tracks are more angular than those of cats and show the prints of their non-retractable claws. They hunt on the ground by night or day.

Except in Labrador, we no longer have the Gray Wolf, that magnificent wild dog that terrorized our ancestors and kept the caribou herds healthy and fleet by pruning the weak and careless. They are gone from our region, perhaps forever. One of the last on Newfoundland's northeast coast was killed by Eliza Goulding Francis in 1869. She had gone to fetch water and found it blocking her path, bloated with salt herring she had left in the water to soak. Dropping her buckets, she grabbed the axe that they used for chopping ice and brained it. Later she and her husband Charlie claimed five English pounds as bounty.

"God's Dog" was the name the Plains Natives gave the Coyote, vowing that it would be the last creature on earth. Certainly few Easterners expected this prairie wolf to turn up here. New Englanders began reporting sightings in the 1930s. In 1966 one was killed by a car near Debec in New Brunswick's Carleton County. By the mid-1970s Nova Scotia sheep farmers acknowledged a new predator. In the 1980s coyotes made it to Prince Edward Island. They even rode drift ice across the Cabot Strait to western Newfoundland.

Besides being a devoted parent, this little wolf's speed, cunning, and adaptability ensures its survival. A swift hunter adept at operating in relays or small packs, it is almost certain to capture anything smaller than a deer, and sometimes even deer. It is common for one coyote to distract a groundhog or chipmunk while another pounces. If prey is scarce or the weather bad, Coyotes will make do with berries, grass, or garbage until things improve. Coyotes have survived attempts by hunters and sheepherders elsewhere to eradicate them. God's Dog is here to stay.

Our smallest wild dog is the Gray Fox, found from southern Maine throughout most of the United States, and recently moving into southeastern Canada. It is a shy forest animal with the distinction of being able to climb trees to catch prey and escape enemies.

The slightly larger Red Fox cannot climb trees, but it is bolder and has other talents. Although its fluffy tail and soft fur exaggerate its size, it is actually not much bigger than a large house cat. Its colour ranges from deep rust through orange-yellow to silvery—glossy black with white guard hairs. While all variations can appear in the same litter, the tail is always white-tipped and the feet

Above: *Breeders have capitalized on the genetic colouration variability of the Red Fox to produce a variety of shades.*

Above: *Red Fox pups are born in litters of four to nine. These two are curious about the big world just outside their den.*

Facing page: *A Coyote in winter coat detects a faint sound.*

and legs always black.

The Red Fox breeds in February. For a den it generally chooses an unused groundhog burrow with a good view. Fox dens smell faintly skunky. Because hawks take the pups by day and owls catch them by night, the pups seldom venture afield until early autumn. Then, with some parental guidance, they strike out. After training on frogs, salamanders, and that staple food, mice, young foxes go on to hares, pheasants, grouse, and sometimes poultry. They also dine on berries, grain, and even grass.

Adult foxes don't den up in winter. Instead they curl up in a ball anywhere that is dry, using the tail as a muff for nose and paws. While a lynx sometimes catches one in deep snow, their worst enemies are internal parasites and diseases such as rabies, distemper, and mange. This skin affliction can leave the animal half bald.

As one would expect from its alert expression, the Red Fox is an intelligent wild creature. It is famous for using tricks and ruses to fool pursuing hounds. Trappers know that unless they take extreme care to disguise their traps and remove all human scent, not only will the bait be stolen but the traps may be sprung.

Unlike the dog family, cats usually hunt alone or in small family groups. They are sprinters, not marathoners. Their standard hunting technique is to stalk within a few jumps and then pounce. Holding on with their sharp claws, they bite through the windpipe, jugular vein, or spinal cord. Their tracks are roundish with the retractable claws not showing. They hunt mostly on the ground and at night.

Two or three large members of the *Felidae*, or wild cats, prowl the eastern woodlands. In pre-settlement days the Eastern Cougar or Mountain Lion, also called "Catamount" or "Indian Devil," was the one to reckon with. Ranging from sea to sea and from Alaska into South America, it was as tall as a German Shepherd and preyed chiefly on moose and deer. Later some became too interested in cattle and sheep. For a century or so it seemed to be extinct in Canada except from the Alberta foothills west; then reports of eastern sightings began to trickle in. Since the 1940s, two hundred reports have been listed for New Brunswick and Nova Scotia, with sixty-one in 1988 alone.

So far there has been no positive proof that this lion exists here, but it probably does. Identifying it wouldn't be difficult. Besides being about three times larger than the average adult Lynx or Bobcat, Cougars are distinguished by their tawny colour and long, drooping tail as thick as a person's arm. The tracks resemble those of a house cat, but measure up to ten centimetres long. Females in heat utter piercing screams similar to those of the Porcupine. Any evidence should be reported as soon as possible to the nearest provincial or state wildlife office.

To "lick one's weight in wildcats" is indeed a feat. For its size the Bobcat is one of nature's most ferocious fighters, as many a hunting dog has discovered. Even kittens raised in captivity seldom become completely trustworthy. But unless cornered or molested it minds its own business.

The Bobcat's prey includes mice, hares, woodchucks, chipmunks, and grouse. Sometimes it manages to kill a deer. Its preferred habitat is woodland with enough openings to provide habitat for small mammals and birds. Like the Lynx it can climb trees.

Bobcats range across the continent from Florida northward in many habitats, provided the snow isn't too deep. It isn't fond of water either.

Above: *Though smaller than the Bobcat, the Lynx seems larger because of its heavy coat and large hind feet that allow it to walk over deep snow. Unlike the Bobcat, it has conspicuous ear tufts and a completely black-tipped tail. Litters average four to nine and are born in April or May in a ground den.*

Facing page: *The "bob" in Bobcat comes from its short tail, which is black- tipped except underneath. Females breed in late winter and average two kittens each spring. They prefer broken brushy woodland with thick under-growth.*

The Bobcat prefers to go the long way around to avoid even a shallow pond. Both parents tend the young and teach them to hunt.

Paler than the Bobcat, Lynx live almost exclusively on Snowshoe Hare. When hare numbers slump or rise, lynx numbers do the same a year later. Deep evergreen forests with brushy openings suit them both. With its high rump the Lynx appears to be perpetually walking downhill. Like its favourite prey, it has long legs and large, furry, hind feet that take it over snow where a Bobcat would flounder. Although family groups may hunt together and meow to maintain contact, this cat is normally a silent loner. Furriers prize its thick, soft, pastel coat. In a trap it seldom struggles; one lynx that was held by only a single talon did not try to escape until the trapper appeared.

The Weasel tribe is named for its smallest member. In descending order of size, other members are the Otter, Fisher, Pine Marten, and Mink. The Striped Skunk, which is omnivorous, is also of this tribe. All share an unmistakable musk produced by twin anal glands, hence their Latin name, *Mustelidae.*

Otters are intelligent, fun loving, and very much at home in fresh water. They can swim more than four hundred metres under water without air. When otters aren't chasing a meal of brook trout or lake perch they may be romping down a mud or snow slide, sun-bathing, or frolicking in a lake. In winter this sleek animal wears a layer of fat like the Seal, which it resembles. Unlike seals, Otters have visible ears and webbed feet that function well on land. When hunting in murky water they rely on a keen nose and highly sensitive whiskers. They eat fish headfirst, spitting out the tail. They also eat clams, insects, and sometimes a muskrat or bird.

Although somewhat awkward out of water, Otters regularly travel overland between streams and lakes, loping over well-worn trails. In winter they seek places that never freeze to enter and leave the water.

Fishers don't fish. The name echoes that of their European relative, the Polecat or *fitchet,* which in turn comes from an old Danish word meaning "to stink." This is unfair, since our Fishers hardly smell at all. Instead of fish, this fox-sized animal eats most woodland mammals that live on or above the ground. This includes the Marten, one of the few mammals fast enough to capture a squirrel. And the Fisher is among the

Above: *This reclusive lion, the Eastern Cougar, was once fairly common here and preyed on moose, deer, and smaller animals. Like all cats, cougars hunt by stalking, sprinting, and pouncing. An adult male weighs up to eighty kilograms. Females are about half as big; they bear one to six kittens every two years, usually in a cave.*

few animals able to kill and eat a porcupine safely; it attacks the quill-less underbelly. When trappers decimated the Fisher for its long, black, silky pelt in the 1920s in New Brunswick and Nova Scotia, the Porcupine thrived. To repopulate the region, government biologists released some Maine Fishers in western Nova Scotia in 1947 and again in the 1960s with evident success.

The Marten is really a Sable. It has the same golden brown pelt as its Siberian cousin, whose fur is so prized by furriers and artists. Wildlife authority Victor Cahalane aptly called it a tree-minded weasel; it is completely at home aloft. Its diet is similar to the much larger Fisher's, but with more attention to mice, birds, insects, and snakes. Like the Fisher it also samples berries and other fruits, and carrion.

Martens prefer undisturbed northern forests of spruce and balsam fir with hollow trees for breeding. They fight a lot and live a mostly solitary life. Because trapping, logging, and wildfire have greatly reduced their numbers, they are completely protected. Newfoundland's subspecies is listed as endangered.

The dark brown Mink smells almost as rank as the Skunk and likes the water almost as much as the Otter. It is fond of Muskrat, sometimes entering their houses, killing a whole colony, and taking over their dens. Slower than the Weasel and its larger kin, Mink catch fish, crayfish, ducks, groundhogs, and mice. Long prized by the fashion industry, wild mink fur has lost status owing to ranching and the anti-trapping movement.

The little Weasel has a reputation for being a mass murderer. If it manages to get into a chicken coop at night, it will go on a killing spree. This is unusual behaviour. In the wild, it kills only what it needs. This intelligent, swift, wiry mammal doesn't hesitate to attack prey many times its own size. My father once watched a duck struggling to take off with one clinging to its neck. After several tries the duck shook off her tormentor, which fell into the water.

Weasels are slender enough to navigate the tunnels of mice, destroying untold numbers. They also eat rabbits, frogs, snakes, and birds, even climbing bushes to reach them.

Despite its bloodthirsty habits and vile smell, the Weasel or Ermine wears a dainty white vest in summer, and in winter turns all white except for its black-tipped tail. It is the only Mustelid to do so, and this coat is prized as the ermine of royal robes. The Weasel's enemies include not only the larger owls and hawks, but house cats. Our three species are the Long-tailed or Common, the Short-tailed or Ermine, and, only in New Brunswick and southward, the Least Weasel.

Right: *Weighing up to fifteen kilograms, Otters travel a circuit of up to fifty kilometres up and down brooks and around lakes and seashores in search of perch, trout, and other fish. They also eat muskrats, birds, and small aquatic life. Owing to delayed conception, female Otters mate one spring and bear their litter of one to five kits almost a year later. In contrast, maturation of the newborn kits takes just over forty days.*

Right: *Like the Otter, Mink are at home in streams and lakes and will readily dive for food. Fish, frogs, and small mammals are their principal fare, but they will also kill muskrats and birds.*

Left: *The eight-kilogram Fisher is equally agile in trees and on land. In addition to porcupines and squirrels, it eats mice, shrews, birds, toads, and nuts. Its litter of one to six young is born in a hollow tree.*

Above: *Our equivalent of the famous Old World Russian Sable is the Pine Marten. Overtrapping and loss of suitable habitat led to a drastic decline in numbers throughout the Northeast in the early 1900s. Attempts are now being made to re-introduce this handsome member of the weasel tribe.*

Left: *Although Weasels live mainly on small mammals found in their forest habitat, they will attack prey many times their size. One was seen dangling from the throat of a duck as the bird tried to get airborne.*

Facing page: *Moles stay underground by day and live mostly on earthworms, insects, millipedes, and other prey that they find on the forest floor and in fields at night. The Star-nosed Mole has distinctive pink nose tentacles for locating food.*

Below: *Because its metabolism is tuned so high, the tiny Shrew must hunt day and night year-round to survive, pausing only for a nap now and then. Its main diet is insects, worms, snails, millipedes, and small vertebrates. Several species prowl the woods, swamps, and fields.*

INSECT-EATERS

Our insect-eaters include Moles, Shrews, and several species of small Bat. The term insectivore, however, properly refers only to Moles and Shrews. Bats are of the Order *Chiroptera* (hand-winged), which includes tropical fruit bats. Moles are miners, Shrews hunt on the surface, and Bats have taken to the air. The ground dwellers have small bodies, narrow snouts, and five-clawed toes.

The Shrew is a little warrior about the size of the thumb of an adult human. It is the smallest of all North American mammals. It is also the most highstrung, having to kill and eat its own weight in meat every three hours to stay alive. As a result, a sixteen-month-old shrew is considered old. Shrews bear musk glands on their flanks to deter predators. Unfortunately for the Shrew, owls and hawks can't smell.

Atlantic Canada has five species, namely the Masked, Smoky, Northern Water, Pigmy, and Short-tailed shrews. Two others, the Long-tailed and Least, occur sparsely in New England. The Short-tailed Shrew secretes a salivary toxin with which it immobilizes prey. When the family cat leaves a shrew on the doorstep, it is usually the Common or Masked Shrew. The Water Shrew swims, dives, and runs about on stream bottoms, its fur shining with silvery air bubbles. It can even walk on water for short distances by holding air bubbles in its paws.

In Atlantic Canada Moles are found only in New Brunswick and Nova Scotia. We have two species, the Hairy-tailed (*Parascalops*) and the Star-nosed (*Condylura*). From Massachusetts south to Florida and west to Minnesota, the Eastern Common Mole (*Scalopus*) is best known. Moles have short legs and strong front claws that equip them well for tunnelling. Their soft fur, which moves forward or backward with ease, allows them to reverse direction comfortably in tight spots. Contrary to popular belief, Moles do not eat the roots of trees and crops. However, they do churn up mounds of earth on lawns in search of insect larvae. They don't hesitate to swim and dive.

Moles spend so much time underground that their eyes and ears are rudimentary. To compensate, their senses of smell and touch are acute. In fact the Star-nosed Mole has a ring of twenty-two sensitive pink tentacles around its nose to help locate the worms and insects on which it feeds. These tentacles, in constant motion while hunt-

Above: *These pregnant Little Brown Bats are huddled together for warmth. In late fall bats home in on ancestral caves and mine shafts where they spend the winter in a deep sleep. In summer, they sleep all day and emerge at dusk from sheltered places such as attics, caves, and from under tree bark to scoop up thousands of night-flying insects like moths and mosquitoes.*

Facing page: *Intelligent, fast, and immensely strong, an adult Black Bear commands respect. Though they rarely harm people, panhandling bruins can become dangerous around garbage dumps and public parks when they lose their instinctive fear of humans.*

ing, are curled inward when it eats. This Mole stores fat in its tail, which is as long as its body and swells to the size of a pencil. An excellent diver and swimmer, it lives as far north as southern Labrador.

Although the Northeast's nine known species of Bats are strictly insectivorous, many tropical species eat fruit. One, the Vampire Bat, lives on blood. Contrary to popular belief, our Bats never drink blood, never get tangled in people's hair, and rarely carry rabies.

Bats are the only mammals capable of free, sustained flight. Although they see well, they depend on echo-location to avoid obstacles and to capture prey. Each species emits characteristic high-pitched sounds from its open mouth and picks up the resulting echoes with oversized ears. Their year is divided in two parts. From autumn to spring, when insects are absent or rare, they migrate by the thousands to traditional hibernation sites in caves or mine shafts. There they become so inert that condensation forms on their fur, while their breathing and heart rate almost cease.

During the warmer months the females seek hot dry havens, like attics, in which to raise their young. While the chirping and clicking of hungry babies and the smelly droppings can be annoying, there are benefits. Each adult bat can eat up to twenty thousand mosquitoes in an evening.

Our more common Bats are the Little Brown, the Keen's Myotis, and the Big Brown (*Eptesicus*). Much rarer are the Hoary, and the Red Bat (*Lasiurus*), the Silver-haired Bat (*Lasionycteris*), Small-footed Myotis, and, smallest of all, the Eastern Pipistrelle (*Pipistrellus*). Western Vermont and Massachusetts have the rare and endangered Indiana Myotis.

OMNIVORES

Just as the domestic cow will chew bones for the calcium in them, most plant-eaters will eat a little meat. Likewise a dog or cat will gnaw grass. This doesn't make any of them omnivores. Omnivores (all-eaters) are opportunists who routinely eat almost anything that comes along—foliage, nuts, berries, freshly killed meat or carrion, insects, fish, birds' eggs, and roots. To handle such a diet they need a variety of dental equipment: chisel teeth for cutting and scraping, canines for piercing, molars for grinding, and scissorlike carnassials for shearing. Humans are politely omnivorous.

The Bear and Raccoon are our classic omnivores. Plants make up most of a Black Bear's food. But it will kill and dine on a lost moose calf or rip open an anthill and lick up the swarming insects. Other common foods vary with the season. In spring it eats various greens, relishing bird and reptile eggs where found; in summer and fall it consumes many fruits, nuts and honey, insects and their eggs, and small animals. Bears also eat garbage, park handouts, and carrion whenever available. A few renegades will prey on sheep and other livestock that are not well protected. All of this food is normally found within a twenty-five-kilometre radius.

An important habitat requirement for Black Bears is a suitable den for hibernation. Each animal seeks a protected place such as a large fallen tree, hollow log, an overhung rock ledge, or even a pile of logging slash. Unless a midwinter thaw arouses them, they stay put until spring. Around February the pregnant sows deliver one to three kitten-sized cubs. Nursing from their sleeping mother, they grow rapidly. When spring comes the family is ready to head out and forage. Adult

Facing page: *This lovable masked character was surprised at night in a tree below its mother and siblings. Usually two to four young are born in spring, after about two months' gestation, in a protected den or hollow tree. The Raccoon's resemblance to a panda bear is not accidental. They are fairly closely related.*

females normally breed every other year; cubs usually tag along until the following summer.

Raccoons are related to Bears, and especially to Old World Pandas, which they resemble. Wooded areas interrupted by fields and watercourses are their favourite habitat, preferably with suitable denning sites such as abandoned woodchuck burrows, dry road culverts, or, best of all, hollow trees. There the females give birth to three to five cubs. Like its large relative, the Raccoon eats a wide range of seasonal animal and plant foods—with more of the former in spring and early summer, and more of the latter toward fall. Typical sources include crustaceans, worms, insects, carrion, tender buds and shoots, grass, fruits and seeds, and human garbage.

These born opportunists learn quickly. Given opportunity, they are adept at petty theft and even door-to-door solicitation. Sometimes people keep them illegally as pets. Although raccoons are cute when young, they can become unruly and even dangerous when mature.

Another omnivore in Atlantic Canada and New England is the Striped Skunk. In spring, the Skunk lives mostly on meadow mice, moles, and shrews. All summer, in exchange for the fruit, honey, and poultry that it may steal, it destroys garden pests and thousands of June bug larvae.

Good qualities notwithstanding, few people want skunks around. "As welcome as a skunk at a garden party," we say. Actually, a skunk never attacks without serious provocation. Even then it stamps its feet and grunts fair warning. If the provocation continues, the little animal flares its tail, hitches its body into a tight U (with the victim held in view over one shoulder), takes aim, and rapidly fires several jets from its twin anal ducks. The thick, oily, amber-coloured liquid

instantly turns to a fine spray. Very accurate to nearly four metres, this jet may travel two more. When shot into a dog's face, the substance temporarily blinds and sends the victim yelping for relief. The odour is extremely difficult to remove.

Like a relic from the past, the tough, opportunistic Opossum prospers in a world of placental mammals. The only marsupial in North America, it belongs to the Order *Marsupialia* whose proper home is Australasia and Central and South America.

Just thirteen days after the female Opossum conceives, up to eighteen wormlike, blind embryos or *neonates* the size of bumble bees leave their mother's cloaca and haul themselves laboriously upward through her coarse fur. If lucky, they find the small opening of her pouch, enter, and fasten onto one of thirteen pin-sized teats. In a month the seven to nine survivors peek out. Two months later, after a spell of piggy-backing on their mother, they are on their own.

Opossums are large and rat-shaped. They dine on anything from insects to garbage, and they prey on mice, moles, and shrews. Opossums range as far north as southern parts of Vermont, New Hampshire, and Maine, but those living farthest north often lose their naked ears and tails to frostbite. They do not fully hibernate.

Facing page: *This smelliest member of the weasel tribe never attacks unprovoked and always gives fair warning. As if the costume wasn't enough, it shuffles its front paws and hoists its tail. Although Skunks sleep most of the winter away, they are not true hibernators and may be seen ambling about during mild spells in search of a mate and food.*

Above: *Stretched out on a grapevine, a Virginia Opossum coils its prehensile tail for a better grip. This omnivore is North America's only animal that carries its developing young in a pouch.*

SEA MAMMALS

A SEAL UNDER WATER LOOKS VERY fishLIKE. ITS webbed feet and streamlined body allow it to dart and twirl with abandon. On land a seal is clumsy. It humps its bulky body along awkwardly. Unlike an otter, it makes little use of its front legs, which are too high up to reach the ground. Much of its bulk consists of a thick layer of blubber or fat. This protects it from the constant chill of the ocean and smooths its body contours.

Most experts agree that whales or cetaceans first appeared some 30 to 50 million years ago. At first glance they look so fishlike that linking them to land mammals seems far-fetched. Yet, whales are warm-blooded and breathe air. Hidden in their pectoral fins are very handlike bones, and some whales even retain vestigial whiskers and hip bones. They mate in the water, bear live young up to one-third their own length, and feed them warm milk from retractable nipples. At one stage their embryos are even furry. Whales and dolphins can stay under water longer than any other mammal.

The whale's adaptations for ocean life are amazing. It can't choke on its food; the closable breathing tube goes directly to the lungs without a throat connection. The cetacean lacks external ears, but hears far better than we do. It sees with a fixed-focus eye which is protected by oily tears and can withstand the immense pressure of deep dives. Unable to swivel its eye or head, it must turn its whole body to look around. Lacking fishlike scales or slime to reduce drag on their huge bodies, whales have an always-shedding, supersensitive skin that constantly compensates for turbulence and allows them to propel their huge bulk through the water at speeds that still baffle physicists. Unlike fish, whose tails are vertical, Whales have powerful horizontal flukes for propulsion, with the front flippers used mainly for balance and turning.

Whales are found in all oceans, and in their global migrations appear to navigate by the earth's electro-magnetic lines of force. They exhibit certain characteristic behaviours such as blowing or spouting (breathing on the surface), breaching (leaping and falling back into water), spyhopping (lifting the head out of water to see better), lobtailing and flipper-slapping (slamming tails or flippers on the ocean with deafening sounds heard two or more kilometres away), logging (lying prone and motionless on the surface, perhaps sleeping), and sounding (diving after a period of blowing).

Sea mammals are essentially carnivorous. All our native seals eat mostly fish and molluscs that they capture along the coast and under offshore ice. Whales, on the other hand, have two different modes of feeding, and are classified on that basis into those with teeth and those with baleen or "whalebone."

Toothed whales eat squid, fish, seals, and, in the case of the Orca, other whales. Like Bats they use echo-location, or sonar, to navigate, find food, and communicate. Some scientists think they use bursts of sound to stun their prey, which they swallow whole.

The baleen whale feeds near the surface by skimming or gulping a mouthful of water filled with small fish, crustaceans, and plankton into its expandable throat. It then uses its tongue to expel the water through strainers hung from the upper jaw, and swallows the meal deposited. These filters consist of strips or plates of whalebone or ker-

Facing page: *Every August and September Gray Seals return to traditional rookeries on the coast of Atlantic Canada to whelp and breed and sun themselves. Those who fish for a living dislike them because, like the Harbor Seal, they carry the parasitic cod worm.*

Facing page: *The young of the Harp Seal are famous for the number that are born and the publicity surrounding the now-banned, traditional, spring seal hunt for their pelts off northeast Newfoundland.*

Below: *The spots that give this seal its nickname "Leopard Seal" are clearly visible as these animals raise their doglike heads for air and a look around. Note as well the tiny ear holes. Other common names for this seal are "Bay Seal" and, in Newfoundland, "Ranger."*

atin—the stuff fingernails are made of and which nineteenth century women wore as corset stays.

Baleen whales sometimes corral fish by diving underneath and expelling a circular curtain of rising bubbles. The largest consume about a tonne of food each day. Despite their huge maws, none can swallow anything bigger than a herring.

Baby whales are normally born after thirty to sixty minutes' labour. They come out tail first with flukes and fins folded, and within ten seconds are helped to the surface to take their first breath. The short umbilical cord has weak points that snap when pulled taut.

SEALS

The four common Seals of the Northeast are the Harbour, Gray, Harp, and Hood. Outside of a wildlife park, most people never see any of them. But nearly every winter our newspapers carry stories about seals crossing highways or being stranded in fields. Almost always these are Harbour Seals taking shortcuts between bodies of water. This species occupies the coast from southern New England to the Arctic. It ordinarily feeds in deep waters but often comes into shallow bays in summer to sun itself on rocks and sandbars at low tide. It also swims up rivers to feed on trout and salmon. Although curious, it dives at the slightest alarm. It rests and breeds on shore.

The Gray Seal also comes to land to breed. One well-known rookery is on Sable Island, 160 kilometres east of Canso, Nova Scotia. About a fortnight after the bulls arrive in September to stake out a small territory, the cows arrive to have their single pups. During the breeding period the female eats little or nothing. Clad in soft white fur at first, the baby grows a new bluish-gray coat within a month. It is then abandoned by its emaciated mother to follow the herd to sea and learn to cope for itself.

The Harp and Hood seals are animals of the far North that migrate to our latitudes to breed. Summering around the Arctic ice floes off Greenland and Labrador, they swim south in the autumn to appear in March on the ice floes off Newfoundland and in the Gulf of St. Lawrence. While the Harps gather in thousands on the main floes, the larger Hoods, weak-clawed and less able to maintain breathing holes, occupy broken ice nearer the outer edge of the pack. The familiar whitecoat pups are the offspring of Harp Seals; Hoods give birth to gray pups.

When whelping is in full swing, the leading edge of the ice pack is often black with seals, and on calm days their loud barking carries for several kilometres. Somehow the mothers, returning from fishing under the drifting ice, manage to find their own pups in the melee. As soon as the pups are weaned, the females abandon them to return north. Untold numbers of pups starve, are crushed by moving floes, or are eaten by Polar Bears, Sharks, and Orcas on their journey north. Despite this and over a century of slaughter, Harps and Hoods are abundant.

Recent protests against seal killing have led to their increasing numbers. This is a concern to those engaged in commercial fishing. Since each adult seal consumes several hundred kilograms of fish each week, they are regarded as serious competitors of limited fish stocks.

TOOTHED WHALES

Toothed Whales have a single blow-hole while baleen whales have two. Females are smaller than males. Toothed whales travel and hunt in tightly knit social groups called pods. The principal toothed whales of northeastern waters are the Sperm, Pigmy Sperm, Porpoise, and Dolphin. Dolphins generally have beaklike snouts and conical teeth, while Porpoises usually have flat teeth and no beak. The Harbour Porpoise is our most common representative of the latter. Among the former are the Bottle-Nosed and Atlantic White-sided dolphins.

Our largest members of the *Delphinidae* are the Pilot Whale (up to six metres) and the Killer Whale (nine metres). Two northern relatives are the Beluga and Narwhal. All have plentiful teeth designed to catch, hold, and carve prey.

Herman Melville's fictional *Moby Dick* was an albino Sperm Whale. Largest of the toothed whales, the Sperm (*Physeter macrocephalus*) was named and prized for the reservoir of fine oil and wax in its head as well as the usual fat. While surpassed in size by the Blue Whale, the Sperm grows to twenty metres and up to fifty tonnes. The female is about half that size. The head of a full-grown bull may be more than two metres high, three metres wide, and six metres long. Most of this consists of the spermaceti organ, a mass of oil-filled connective tissue surrounded by muscle and blubber. Containing up to four tonnes of the finest oil, it is thought to control the animal's buoyancy through heating and cooling. Ambergris, a waxy concretion formed in the bowels of Sperms only, is prized in the perfume and drug trades and was once worth more than gold.

An adult bull's underslung, five-metre-long jaw has twenty-four to thirty conical teeth, each up to eighteen centimetres long and weighing nearly a kilogram. They fit into sockets in the toothless upper jaw. The Sperm's dark gray skin looks shrunken and corrugated and is up to thirty-six centimetres thick on its back. After blowing a distinctive, forty-five degree leftward spout from its S-shaped blowhole every ten to thirty seconds for fifteen minutes or more, the whale dives to feed.

Its chief food is squid of many species and sizes. One Sperm was found with twenty-eight thousand cuttlefish beaks in its stomach. On its deepest dives of perhaps two kilometres, it captures giant squid known to grow up to thirteen metres long. Stones, crabs, sand, glass fishing buoys, and the odd shoe are often found in the stomachs of captured Sperm Whales. This suggests that they may also grub on the bottom with their slender jaws. Well they might, for they need from one to one and a half tonnes of food each day.

Facing page: *The Orca or so-called Killer Whale, the ocean's most fearsome predator, is actually a dolphin. It travels in tightly knit family groups or pods, maintaining contact, and identifying each other by body markings and complex clicks and other sounds. They prey on seals, fish, and other whales.*

Facing page: *Until one witnesses it, the Humpback Whale's feat of heaving its sixty-tonne body almost clear of the water is difficult to believe. Humpbacks routinely engage in such seemingly playful behaviour. Some believe the impact may help rid the animal of marine lice and barnacles.*

In one documented case in the Pacific in 1820, a large bull rammed the whaler *Essex* and sank it after members of the pod were harpooned. Considered by whalers to be cunning and resourceful, this animal has the largest brain of any living creature, and larger than that of any Baleen whale. It weighs up to nine kilograms. Because of this whale's deep-water habits we know little of its actual intelligence. Underwater microphones have picked up a great deal of vocal interaction, but nobody knows what it means. Females gather in "nursing pods" in tropical and temperate waters, while young and mature males form "bachelor pods" that roam cooler waters. Calves are about four metres long when born.

Despite heavy hunting by Yankee whalers in the eighteenth century, it is the most common of the great whales today, with over a million individuals worldwide. Sperm Whales are thought to live seventy or more years.

Pigmy Sperms, which reach only four metres, are seldom seen or hunted.

Although Sperm Whales are the world's largest predators, the Orca or Killer Whale rules the oceans. Humans are its only enemy. Usually found in cool coastal waters, this striking black-and-white dolphin with the erect triangular fin up to two metres high travels in close-knit pods or family groups and preys on fish, birds, seals, and even other whales.

Far more intelligent and powerful than sharks, Orcas seem to like the company of humans and are easily trained in captivity. Their reputation as bloodthirsty killers is undeserved. Although fully capable of sinking small boats and with ample motive for revenge, they have never been known to kill a human. In fact they have been known to help people in distress. The rare recorded attacks were probably cases of mistaken identity.

Occasionally, Pilot or Pothead Whales beach themselves in bays and estuaries and die. Towed to sea, they stubbornly return. This phenomenon, common to most whales, has puzzled people for years. Now scientists believe that the strandings relate to anomalies in the earth's electro-magnetic field by which whales seem, in part, to navigate.

Dolphins and Porpoises, among the most intelligent and playful of marine mammals, appear to enjoy the company of ships. On an ocean voyage, pods of these acrobats can often be seen racing the bow wave or pirouetting in spectacular leaps. Highly sociable, they team up to catch fish and to protect each others' young. They have even been known to protect swimmers from sharks.

Dolphins and Porpoises have an astounding hearing capacity. They can distinguish up to 150,000 cycles per second. Humans only hear up to 16,000 cycles.

BALEEN WHALES

Our common Baleen Whales are the Right, Fin, Minke, and Humpback. Until a ban was imposed in 1967, the Blue, a northern species, was decimated by overhunting. It is seldom seen today. All are globe trotters, the Atlantic Blue ranging from Greenland to Newfoundland, the others from the North Atlantic to the tropics.

Baleen whales are filter-feeders distinguished by double nostrils, whalebone plates of various sizes and colours in the upper jaw (thus the family name *Mysticetae* or "moustached"), and expandable pleats that run lengthwise from chin to navel. Unlike toothed whale females, baleen cows average larger than males.

Whalers gave the Right Whale of the Arctic this name because it has thicker blubber, is slow

moving and easy to catch, and does not sink when killed. Also, its widely spaced blowholes create a V-shaped spout that is easy to spot at a distance. It averages fifteen metres long and weighs about fifty-five tonnes.

Some modern whale-watchers have trouble determining how the parts of its head fit together. Curving up from a relatively tiny eye and out under its tapering snout is a huge scoop of a mouth hung with finely fringed black baleen. (A view of the curved lips from the front has earned a relative the name of Bowhead.) Even more odd are the whitish growths called callosities where eyebrows, moustache, and goatee might be.

Infestations with whale lice and sometimes barnacles also form patterns that allow scientists to identify individual animals. Although very rotund, the Right Whale is fairly acrobatic. It feeds by cruising slowly near the surface with its mouth open, skimming vast numbers of tiny crustaceans and plankton. The young are born five to six metres long in warm waters and stay with the mother for a year. Protected since 1937, this species is still the most endangered of great whales. It lives to be about forty years of age.

Somewhat more graceful is the Humpback that congregates in spring and fall near the Fundy and Atlantic shores to fatten for its 3,300-kilometre journey to tropical waters. Its winglike front fins, which are one-third as long as its body and distinctly patterned with white markings beneath and scalloped forward edges, make the species unmistakable and identify individuals, as well.

The Humpback is known as the "songster of the sea." Its unearthly medley of moans, wails, and clicks, first recorded in the 1970s, has won the hearts of thousands. Certain Humpbacks, nicknamed friendlies, are curious about boats and humans and will come to show off their calves or to have their chins scratched. Though huge, they are very acrobatic and playful. They repeatedly leap almost clear of the water and engage in a repertoire of other whale activities such as lobtailing, flipper-slapping, and even what seems to be deliberate spraying of onlookers. Humpbacks also engage in "bubble-net feeding," that is, they release bubbles while swimming upward to corral fish and krill. Occasionally Humpbacks wander far up rivers, then return to sea. They live for forty-five to fifty years, average fifteen metres long and thirty to fifty tonnes.

Slimmer than the Right and Humpback, the Blue, Fin, and Minke whales are streamlined and speedy members of the Baleen group. Said to be the mightiest of all creatures that have lived on earth, the Blue must be described in superlatives. An adult weighs 80 to 120 tonnes, and when spyhopping stands as tall as a ten-story building. Its heart is as big as a compact car and pumps a stream of blood through an aorta as wide as a sewer cover. The open mouth measures more than six metres long, nearly five metres high, and three metres wide. Yet, its throat, like that of all Baleen whales, barely admits a herring. In contrast a Sperm can swallow a shark or a person, and an Orca can down a walrus.

For all its bulk the Blue gives the impression of delicacy with its softly mottled grayish-blue shading above which changes to yellowish-white below, earning it the nickname "Sulphur-Bottom." Adult Blues eat about four tonnes of food daily and calve every two or three years. Newborns are nearly eight metres long, drink about five hundred litres of rich milk a day, and gain more than ninety kilograms daily. Extremely endangered from heavy exploitation, especially

from 1883 to 1915, they are thought to number a few hundred in the North Atlantic and a few thousand in the Pacific. At such low populations, meeting and mating become problematical and their future is uncertain.

The Fin or Finback Whale resembles the Blue but is slightly smaller, darker on the back, and whiter underneath. Some individuals have a whitish chevron across the back behind the head. Hunted avidly for decades, it has the dubious distinction of being the first to be taken with the harpoon gun perfected in 1868 by Norwegian Svend Foyn.

Seen from the front, Fin Whales appear to wear a perpetual smile on their tapered, beaklike snouts. They also sport a few whiskers above and below the mouth. Oddly, the baleen plates, which are up to a metre long, shade from dark into white on the right side, echoing the colours of the lower jaw, which is light on the right and dark on the left. Like the Blue, our Finbacks winter in temperate and subtropical waters and summer near Greenland in the Davis Strait.

The Minke, though it may reach more than ten metres, is small by baleen whale standards. Its small, whitish baleen plates are fringed with snow-white bristles, and the northern variety usually features a whitish band across each flipper. Lively and fast, they take an interest in boats and people and often put on a display. Once bypassed by whalers pursuing the larger Blue and Fin whales, Minkes have since come under attack as the Blue and Fin whales have become scarce and protected.

Facing page: *Poking the snout above water while standing on its tail, a Humpback swivels its body to survey the horizon both above and below the water surface. The "stove bolt" bumps are characteristic of this species.*

BIRDS

TRY TO IMAGINE A WORLD WITHOUT BIRDS— no springtime Robins, no Gulls shadowing the summer ferry crossing, no autumn V of honking Geese far overhead, no clamour of Crows on a winter morning. We couldn't even say, "Birds of a feather flock together," or "As wise as an owl."

Like mammals, birds are warm-blooded. Yet, they have scaly legs and lay shelled eggs like reptiles. Unlike either (except the Bat), they are capable of true, sustained flight. In fact no other animal can fly so fast or so far. Their adaptations for flight include paper-thin bones, air sacs, lightweight beaks instead of jaws, and a tailless rump. Unable to chew, they swallow pebbles to grind their food in a muscular organ called the gizzard.

Feathers are their greatest asset. Made of keratin, the material of whale baleen and human fingernails, they are very specialized. The larger wing feathers consist of a strong but lightweight tubular shaft edged with about a hundred twin rows of hairlike filaments with hooks that zip together to create a single elongated vane. Overlapped on either side by hundreds of other vanes, and moved up and down by enlarged chest muscles attached to a deep central keel, the wings easily lift the lightweight body. In-flight control is achieved by flexing various muscles along the modified forearm. Tail feathers steer and brake the hurtling body, and smooth plumage lessens air resistance.

Feathers insulate better than fur. This is important because flying takes a great deal of energy, which is why birds are hot-blooded. While the outer feathers are waterproof, the downy inner ones trap heat next to the skin. With a layer of fat inside, Penguins survive in the Antarctic year-round. Feather coats also make excellent banners to signal one's identity and intentions. But they are not without problems. The wear on feathers is so great that birds must replace them at least once a year; Ptarmigan in subarctic regions moult three times. Preening— adjusting ruffled feathers and realigning barbules that have come unzipped—is a daily chore.

Most birds have a large oil gland at the base of the tail to replace the oil lost while flying or swimming. They pick up the oil on their beaks and rub it over the feathers. Cormorants lack this gland and must dry themselves with outspread wings after diving. To discourage fleas and lice, birds take dust baths and like "anting." With a live ant held in its beak, a bird will probe its skin or even sit with raised feathers on an active anthill. Ants exude formic acid which lice dislike.

Wings are shaped according to their function. The speedy Swallows and Falcons have narrow, tapered wings; slower flyers like Grouse and some Hawks have broad rounded wings for fast turns and braking; high gliders like Gulls and Osprey have wide spans. Only one, the Hummingbird, can hover and fly backwards and sideways.

The form of a bird's beak is also revealing. Short, stubby beaks like those of Grouse and Finch are for cracking seeds. Short, pointed bills are adapted for snatching and holding insects. Long, straight beaks act as wood chisels; long, curving bills function as sensitive probes. The spearlike beaks of Heron and Kingfisher are good for grabbing fish, while the curved hooks of Owls and Hawks allow them to tear tough skin and meat.

Besides being superbly adapted for locomotion and feeding, birds can navigate across trackless oceans, forests, and deserts by landmarks, celestial bodies, and the earth's electro-magnetic field.

Facing page: *Rising in unison, a flock of Sandpipers dazzles the eye as hundreds of the small birds wheel and dip without collisions. Some biologists think this behaviour helps foil predators such as falcons.*

Above: *A Ruffed Grouse chick, hatched in spring from one of the nine to twelve buffy eggs laid in a hollow, hides among dense horsetail and fireweed. The characteristic neck feathers that give it its name lie flat. In winter these birds forage mainly on berries and tree buds, notably those of aspen.*

Facing page: *Noted for its tameness, a Spruce Grouse ventures into a sunny clearing in search of greens and berries. These birds spend most of the time in dense evergreen forests, and in winter forage mainly on the buds of spruce and fir.*

They build nests that vary from the Eagle's massive platform of sticks to the Hummingbird's tiny cup. Birds are colourful, vocal, and important members of the region's fauna. Without them life would be dull indeed. They prey on everything from other birds to insects. While some, like the Passenger Pigeon and Labrador Duck, have been extirpated, and others are threatened by pollution and habitat change, many others have benefited from human activity and in turn benefit us.

LAND BIRDS

ALTHOUGH ALL BIRDS IN THE NORTHEAST UTILIZE moist or wet habitats, most land birds have no use for open water. Instead they occupy a variety of habitats on the ground, in shrubs and trees, and on barren uplands. Some have highly specialized needs. For example, the rare Pileated Woodpecker nests in large dead or dying trees. As logging and forest fires depleted large trees, the bird's numbers dwindled.

Learning to identify birds is a daunting task. Close-up sightings are few, and much has to be inferred from their songs. In most cases only the male birds have bright markings; the nesting female is naturally inconspicuous. Moreover, most songbirds change colouration from spring to fall.

Our common land birds comprise some forty families. The largest of these are the *Parulidae* (Wood Warblers), *Fringillidae* (Grosbeaks, Sparrows, Finches) and *Icteridae* (Blackbirds and allies). Making a complete list of local birds is difficult because most of them visit us only in summer, preferring to winter farther south. Some, like the Cardinal, are merely transients. A few others are accidental, lost or driven off course. Dedicated bird-watchers spend many enjoyable hours figuring all this out.

Grouse and Ptarmigan, of which we have two species each, are wild versions of the familiar barnyard fowl of Asian ancestry. The Ruffed Grouse frequents temperate forests throughout the Northeast. It is well-known as a game bird in the fall and for drumming the air with rapid wingbeats in the spring. Greens, buds, seeds, insects, and berries are its main food. Its explosive break from cover usually startles predators and hunters sufficiently to ensure a getaway. The

Spruce Grouse prefers dense coniferous woods. Its winter staple is conifer buds and needles; in summer it eats insects, fruits, seeds, and mushrooms. The nickname "Fool Hen" comes from its notable tameness, which has saved many a lost person from starvation. Both grouse are year-round residents across Canada, but Spruce Grouse are absent from Anticosti, Prince Edward Island, the Magdalens, and insular Newfoundland. They are found in northern New England, however.

Willow and Rock ptarmigan are northern relatives that turn white in winter. They frequent open tundra and rocky hills from Newfoundland to British Columbia, but are absent in the Maritimes and southward. Summer fare includes insects and greens; in winter they turn to frozen cranberries and buds of dwarf birch and willow. Willow Ptarmigan were introduced to Scatarie Island off Sydney, Nova Scotia in 1970 but fared poorly.

The large, Asian Ring-necked Pheasant and the Hungarian or Gray Partridge are farmland birds introduced to the Northeast and elsewhere in the nineteenth century. They thrive where hedgerows and unharvested or spilled grain are abundant and snows not too deep. Even so, after blizzards or ice storms they sometimes approach human dwellings in search of food. A native bird similar in habits and appearance to the Gray Partridge is the little Bobwhite Quail, found from southern New England to Guatemala.

Wild Turkey, a native woodland species formerly common from New England and southern Ontario to West Virginia, has been restocked in New England with some success. It feeds mainly on nuts.

Owls and Hawks prefer their meat freshly killed. They are the night and day shift in the war against rodents—a fact which helps people forgive them when they steal the odd chicken. All are superb predators armed with strong talons and hooked beaks for holding and tearing prey. While mice are a staple for all, larger members like the Great Horned Owl, Goshawk, and Peregrine Falcon take Snowshoe Hare, Grouse, and Ducks, respectively. The Great Horned Owl even kills an occasional Skunk or Porcupine. Owls swallow small prey whole, later regurgitating and dropping the fur and bones as compact "owl pellets" under their roosts and nests. Owls nest from January onward in the Northeast. Usually female birds of prey are larger than the males; otherwise they look identical. Hawks often use tall dead trees as lookout posts. Most Owls spend the day hunched asleep in dense conifer crowns.

To any small listening mammal, the unearthly nighttime *Hoo-hoo-hoo* of the Great Horned Owl is a portent of murder. Gliding soundlessly on great soft-feathered wings, it is one of our most powerful birds of prey. All our six resident native Owls are night or dusk hunters, seeking prey by sight and sometimes by heat sensing. Except the Barred Owl, which has dark brown irises, all have striking yellow or golden eyes that they can blink independently.

The largest is the Great Horned Owl—Cat Owl in Newfoundland—named for its prominent ear tufts; the smallest is the Saw-whet, from its call's resemblance to the monotonous sound of a mill saw being filed. The others are the Barred, Long-eared, Short-eared, and Hawk owls. The latter is a northern bird usually absent in Nova Scotia and southern New Brunswick in summer, while the Long-eared and Barred are rare or absent from insular Newfoundland. In years when Arctic Lemmings are scarce, we are visited by the

Facing page: *The male Ring-neck Pheasant, a gorgeous bird, has a tail nearly fifty centimetres long. These Asian birds introduced to the Northeast in the nineteenth century are now common in Massachusetts but rare to the north. Ample grain and fairly mild winters are essential for their survival. The drab brown female lays six to fifteen olive brown eggs and may raise two broods a year.*

Facing page: *Though as large as the Great Horned Owl, the Barred Owl seems smaller because it lacks the conspicuous ear tufts. This is the only common owl with brown eyes. The female lays two to three white eggs in early April, usually in a hollow tree.*

Left: *The Short-eared Owl is of medium size and hunts mostly at dawn and dusk in open meadowlands, marshes, and dunes where mice and voles abound. The nest, often sheltered by a bush, is made of coarse grass and weed stems on the ground. In May the female lays four to eight white eggs that hatch around mid-June.*

Below: *The Marsh Hawk or Northern Harrier is an efficient hunter of mice and other small mammals as well as little birds, frogs, and insects. White-rumped and slightly larger than a crow, it is usually seen skimming marshes and meadows in gull-like flight.*

Facing page: *Thanks to painstaking rehabilitation programs by government and volunteer agencies, the endangered Peregrine Falcon or Duck Hawk is slowly recovering in some areas of the Northeast. At normal population levels one pair per five thousand square kilometres was average.*

Overleaf left: *The eye of this Bale Eagle can spot a small fish from a kilometre or more away. The powerful beak is shaped to tear into tough hides and slippery fish.*

Overleaf right: *Like Eagles, Ospreys add to and use the same nest for years. Typically, they raise three young which normally fly at eight to ten weeks. Both parents tend the nest.*

strikingly beautiful Snowy Owl from Ungava and the Arctic islands; the Great Gray and Boreal owls may also appear.

Unlike owls, hawks and falcons hunt by day.Our hawks consist of four Accipiters or true hawks—Northern Goshawk, Sharp-shinned, Cooper's, and Northern Harrier or Marsh Hawk, and four Buteos, namely the Red-shouldered, Red-tailed, Broad-winged, and Rough-legged. All breed here but, with the exception of the Red-tailed, they are uncommon to rare in winter. In general the Accipiters are slight of build with short, rounded wings and longish tails, while the Buteos are stocky with broad, rounded wings and tails. Occasionally other hawks pass through our region.

Falcons have long, slender wings and notched beaks. Three species breed in the Northeast, namely the rare Peregrine or Duck Hawk, the American Kestrel or Sparrow Hawk, and the Merlin or Pigeon Hawk. All are very swift and capable of catching birds in flight. In fact at 130 kilometres per hour (clocked during a power dive) the Peregrine is North America's fastest bird. Once near extinction through habitat destruction and use of DDT, numbers of this crow-sized falcon are increasing thanks to careful breeding and transplant programs. It prefers open country near cliffs. Our smaller falcons prey on mice, small birds, and insects such as grasshoppers.

Our two largest hawklike birds of prey are the Bald Eagle and the Osprey; Golden Eagles are infrequent transients. While Bald Eagles are rare and endangered in New England, Atlantic Canada has the largest breeding population in the Northeast, especially on Cape Breton Island. Many even overwinter. Indeed, in recent years, Nova Scotia has regularly live-trapped eaglets and

shipped them to be raised and released or "hacked" in Massachusetts to help restore the New England population. While eagles make fish their staple diet, they are not averse to a meal of carrion.

Our only true fish hawk is the Osprey. Its long, curved talons and rough foot pads easily hold slippery prey like live eels and flounder, which it seizes by diving into the water. Sometimes the more powerful eagle forces the osprey to relinquish its catch while in flight. Both species mate for life, returning yearly to repair their massive nests. These are built of sticks in tall, shoreline trees near good fishing sites. Where suitable trees are lacking, ospreys will nest on the crossbars of power poles.

Though common in New England in summer, the large Turkey Vulture is rarely seen in the Atlantic provinces. However, it is spreading northeastward. With its naked head and shaggy feathers, it is unmistakable. Except for some plant food, dead meat is its staple. This diet performs a service not only to the environment, but also to the motoring public.

Though no relation to any of the above, the robin-sized Shrike is, nonetheless, a predator of small rodents, birds, and, in summer, insects. Lacking the strong grasping talons of hawks and owls, it impales its prey on thorns or barbed wire before eating.

Facing page: *The Blue Jay is a colourful, loud-voiced cousin of the Crow and western magpie. It is a welcome though sometimes overly aggressive visitor to winter feeders. Its plainer relative the Gray Jay or Whisky Jack is much more reclusive.*

Below: *A Raven is seen foraging on spilled grain. These year-round residents also consume small mammals (mostly carrion such as road kills), insects, nestlings, and fruit in season. They are more solitary than Crows.*

PERCHING BIRDS

BY FAR THE LARGEST NUMBER OF BIRDS WORLD-wide belong to the Order *Passeriformes* or perching birds. Their breeding range in Atlantic Canada alone boasts about one hundred species. Ranging from the tiny Chickadee to larger birds like the Robin and Raven, they include our most colourful, melodious, and interesting birds.

It is difficult to imagine the autumn countryside without Crows cawing and Blue Jays screaming. As the leaves fall and winter approaches, finding food becomes more difficult for these resident birds. One solution is to include carrion or dead meat in their diet. Three of our four members of the Corvidae—Common Crow, Raven, and Gray Jay—regularly do this. A familiar sight along our highways is that of a Crow or Raven pecking at a dead porcupine, and trappers often find the pelt of a caught fox or rabbit ruined by a hungry Gray Jay.

Crows are very sociable. Often they travel in large flocks, morning and evening, between a town dump and a communal roost. They also gather in noisy flocks to heckle the larger owl if they discover one in the open during the day. Crows and Blue Jays are noted for eating grains, fruit, and, in spring, eggs and nestlings. Crows also devour untold numbers of Meadow Voles and weed seeds. While Crows and Blue Jays thrive around mixed farmland and woodlots, Ravens and Gray Jays favour less disturbed areas.

All are intelligent birds with a variety of calls. It is not unusual to see a solitary Raven soaring high, doing barrel rolls, tumbles, and dives, and uttering dry croaks and bell-like notes. People have trained Crows and Ravens to speak a limited vocabulary. Sometimes one sees a flock of both disputing with a Bald Eagle over a carcass; the Eagle always wins.

The Gray Jay or Moose Bird is as quiet as the Blue Jay is brash and noisy. In the woods it will investigate chopping or other sounds, looping closer on silent wings and sometimes it will feed from one's hand. It pilfers camp food, caching the surplus by first coating it with a saliva that hardens like a plastic wrapper. Moose will allow this bird to land on them and remove ticks. Indeed, its nickname, Whisky-jack, is a corruption of an Algonquian word meaning "one who directs hunter to moose."

Without the Chickadee, Nuthatch, and

Creeper, our trees would swarm with insects every summer. All three are indefatigable little bug-eaters year-round. Veteran ornithologist W. Earl Godrey, author of *The Birds of Canada*, called the Chickadee "the personification of cheerfulness." In the worst winter weather, small troupes of these fluffy gray elves may be heard and seen moving from tree to tree, hunting for insect eggs, calling *Chick-a-dee-dee.* They are among the easiest birds to attract to feeders.

Like the Chickadee, the Red-breasted Nuthatch commonly nests in a decaying stump or tree cavity. It has a nasal *nyak, nyak, nyak* that carries far. While Nuthatches usually search a tree trunk head downward, the Brown Creeper works up the trunk in little hitches.

Wrens are tiny, energetic, brownish birds that hold their short tails erect or over their backs. They are mainly insect-eaters, but feed on the ground as well. Of the five species in the Northeast, the Winter Wren breeds throughout. The House and Marsh wrens breed from the Maritimes south, and the Carolina Wren occurs only in southern New England. Noted ornithologist Robie Tufts in his book, *The Birds of Nova Scotia*, called the Winter Wren's song "remarkable for its volume, duration and variation," adding that the singer is far more often heard than seen.

When we say "songbird" most of us mean thrushes, warblers and sparrows. The familiar American Robin is a thrush. Most rural dwellers know the liquid summer serenade of the Yellow Warbler. And one of the first woodland birdsongs many of us learn is the clear, repeated song of the White-throated Sparrow. These three groups embrace most of the perching birds that fill our woods and fields with melody and colour each spring. Although some members overwinter here, most migrate from the southern United States, the Caribbean, and even South America. From mid-March through mid-summer, they bring our landscapes to life.

Among the earliest arrivals are male Robins; in parts of Newfoundland both sexes even overwinter by feeding on mountain ash berries. Early settlers simply named this friendly bird after Europe's beloved Robin Red-breast, a much smaller and unrelated species. Robins are among those birds that benefit from human activity; they frequent logged or burnt forests and open fields and lawns.

Our other common thrushes—the Hermit,

Below: *Though normally patrolling the bark of coniferous trees for insect eggs and larvae, the tiny Red-breasted Nuthatch sometimes gets blown astray during migration. This one came down on the Prince Edward Island-Nova Scotia ferry.*

Swainson's, and Veery—are slightly smaller, and clothed in the soft browns and grays of their forest habitat. All have spotted breasts, lay bluish eggs in bowl-shaped nests of vegetation, and feed mostly on insects and fruit. The silvery, flutelike twilight song of the Hermit Thrush is one of the finest heard in our woodlands, rivalling that of its European cousin the Nightingale.

Close kin to the thrushes, the lovely Eastern Bluebird commonly bred from southern Saskatchewan to Newfoundland, south to Florida. But in recent years it has largely been ousted by the Starling, an aggressive Old World species that arrives earlier and usurps favoured Bluebird nest-

ing sites such as old Woodpecker nests or tree cavities.

Warblers are the despair of novice bird identifiers. Firstly, some two dozen members of the *Parulidae* breed in the Northeast. Secondly, although many are brightly coloured, the breeding plumage of males and females of the same species not only differs, but changes in autumn; that of the juveniles is different again. Moreover, warblers are small, busy creatures that often feed at treetop level. Fortunately, their songs aid in identification, at least during mating and nesting; by mid-summer these birds fall mostly silent.

All have sharp pointed bills and snap up hordes

Right: In spring, males arrive first to stake out nesting and feeding territory. Some weeks later the females follow. Robin are actually thrushes, related to the Nightingale of Europe.

Above: *With its black face mask and gold chain, the male Common Yellowthroat is unmistakable. The similar-looking female nests on or near the ground in low shrubbery, laying three to five whitish eggs that hatch in about twelve days.*

Facing page: *On a sunny day the male Yellow Warbler adds a spot of colour and a song to the sparse spring foliage. This small songster breeds from the Pacific to the Atlantic, favouring ornamental shrubbery around homes and gardens. Like most warblers, the female is drab to camouflage her on the nest.*

of insects; they also sample weed seeds and fruit. Most nest near or on the ground, but the Northern Parula hollows out a hanging clump of beard lichen, and the Blackburnian nests high in conifers. All but two, the tiny Golden-crowned and Ruby-crowned kinglets, belong to strictly New World families. This partial list of the warblers having trans-Canadian ranges suggests the family's diversity: Magnolia, Yellow, Tennessee, Black-and-White, Black-throated Green, Bay-breasted, Blackpoll, Palm, Ovenbird, Northern Waterthrush, Common Yellowthroat, Mourning, American Redstart.

Of these the Mourning is uncommon in Atlantic Canada. The Orange-crowned is mostly confined to Labrador. Our most common warblers are the Black-and-White, Cape May, American Redstart, Ovenbird, Yellowthroat, Bay-breasted, Chestnut-sided, Yellow-rumped (formerly Myrtle), Northern Parula, Nashville, Black-throated Green, and Canada Warbler.

Transients and rare migrants include the Pine, Hooded, Wilson's, Scarlet Tanager, and Prothonotary. Naturally in New England, many of these are more common; but the lovely Cerulean Warbler (*Dendroica*) is locally common only in the Champlain Valley.

Most warblers are gone by October, but the Golden-crowned Kinglet winters with us, tinkling its sleigh-bell song as it forages in the tops of spruce and fir.

Fringillidae is the lovely name for our largest family of birds, to which belong the Grosbeaks, Finches, Sparrows, and Buntings. While nestlings are fed almost exclusively on insects, the badge of this group is the thick strong bill with which they crush their principal food, weed seeds. In many species the cutting edge of the lower mandible is angled downward near its base for greater shearing power.

By far the most glamorous member of the family is the scarlet and black Northern Cardinal, which sometimes strays into the Maritimes from central New England. Next most colourful are the Rose-breasted, Pine, and Evening Grosbeaks (literally, "big-beaks"). Except in Newfoundland, all are common winter visitors in our region. According to Robie Tufts the Evening Grosbeak may have replaced the Rose-breasted (which was called "Winter Robin" because of its dependability and the male's rosy colour) by competing for the same foods.

The Newfoundland Pine Grosbeak, locally called "Mope" for its lethargic habits, is a slightly smaller variant. Similar to the Evening Grosbeak but smaller and far more common is the black and lemon-yellow American Goldfinch. This fairly common summer resident and frequent visitor has a duller, greenish-gray plumage in winter.

Two other common finches are the striped Purple Finch and the Common Redpoll. The latter is a northern bird that breeds south to Newfoundland, visiting the Maritimes in winter, sometimes in large twittering flocks. It is closely related to the brownish Pine Siskin and the American Goldfinch. Our two species of Crossbill, the Red and the White-winged, are named for their crossed upper and lower mandibles, with which they dexterously extract conifer seeds, often hanging upside down and using bill and feet like parrots. Both species have a circum-polar range in coniferous forests, are highly nomadic, and are known to nest here in any month of the year.

Even windswept Sable Island has sparrows—in fact a distinctly paler and larger subspecies of the

mainland Savannah Sparrow has evolved among the dunes and marram grass. Called the Ipswich Sparrow after its winter home in Massachusetts, it is living proof, says Nova Scotia author Thomas Raddall, that this tiny crescent of sand has been there a long time. It also attests to the endurance and navigational skills of even small birds.

Although many species of sparrows breed in or visit the Northeast, in summer the most common are the White-throated, Swamp, Song, Savannah, and Chipping sparrows. In Labrador the White-crowned is more evident. All are small, energetic, brown and gray birds with sturdy beaks and distinctive chestnut, yellow, or white markings, depending on the bird. The Fox Sparrow is more common as a spring and fall transient. On its autumn migration it likely follows the New Brunswick shore, crossing the Bay of Fundy to Nova Scotia before continuing south.

Perhaps the best known, if not the best sparrow songster, is the White-throated, whose plaintive melody has been likened in Canada to "I love Canada-Canada-Canada," and in the United States to "Old Sam Peabody-Peabody-Peabody." Several of these species reside year-round in southern New England.

Two of the most common sparrow-related winter visitors are the Slate-coloured Junco, known as "Split-tail" in Newfoundland, and the Snow Bunting. The latter was the inspiration for songwriter Gene MacLellan's hit melody, "Snowbird," made famous by Anne Murray. The Snow Bunting breeds in the treeless Arctic, and, true to its name, usually arrives in chirping flocks before the first heavy snowfall and leaves before the snowbanks have melted. People marvel that their arrival so often coincides with the first snowstorm. Actually, during open winters they stay along our

Above: *A rosy-tinted male Pine Grosbeak and his grayer companion—either a female or a juvenile male—feed on high bush cranberries in mid-winter. Its song resembles that of a Robin, but is faster and more energetic. The nest is usually made of twigs and old man's beard lichen, and lined with fine grass or fur.*

Facing page: *The brown stripe that gives the Chestnut-sided Warbler its name is clearly visible on this male. The plainer female lays three to five speckled white eggs in a nest of fine grass and weed materials a metre or less above ground.*

coastal lowlands, but the first blizzard usually drives them inland to scour farmlands for weed seeds and grain. Sometimes they travel with the Horned Lark, a somewhat similar northern transient.

The ubiquitous, cheeping House or English "Sparrow" is actually a weaver finch from Europe, a family with no New World counterpart. Introduced to Brooklyn, New York in 1850 and later to Halifax, Nova Scotia, and Quebec City, Quebec, it now resides from coast to coast. An aggressive bird that thrives around humans, it often dominates winter feeders. Since it starts nesting around February, it usurps the habitat of native cavity-nesting birds such as Tree and Bank Swallows that arrive later. Sometimes it drives Cliff Swallows from their mud nests.

Icteridae is an interesting New World family comprising Blackbirds, Meadowlarks, and Orioles. The Rusty Blackbird and the longer-tailed Bronzed Crow-Blackbird are common to the Northeast. The Common Grackle with its lovely iridescent blue-purple neck and the Red-winged Blackbird breed only as far east as the western part of Newfoundland. The sparrowlike Bobolink with its distinctive yellow, black, and white colouration is not found east of Cape Breton. One species, the Cowbird, imitates Old World Cuckoos by laying its eggs in the nests of other birds.

Two uncommon transients are the Eastern Meadowlark, which breeds sparingly in the Northeast, and the "Golden Robin" or Northern Oriole, common in New England but rare here. The latter is noted for its durable hanging baglike nest; the former nests in hayfields but is not a Lark.

With its sailor's gait and dark plumage, the Common Starling resembles a blackbird as it inspects the lawn for seeds and insects. But it is as European as the House Sparrow, having been introduced to New York City in 1890. Unlike the blackbird it has a stubby tail, yellow bill, and iridescent blue, green, and purple plumage in the summer. A cavity nester, it often usurps the place of native birds such as Kestrels and Northern Flickers.

Flycatchers catch insects from a sitting start. Atop a telephone pole by an open field a Kingbird waits patiently. Then, with a spring it intercepts its prey, snaps, and returns to its perch to enjoy the catch. Its smaller cousin, the Phoebe, pursues the same trade near cliffs and streamside clearings, and the still smaller Olive-sided Flycatcher and Eastern Wood-Pewee hawk from treetops. The tiny Yellow-bellied Flycatcher hunts in deep, damp, coniferous woods.

"Swallows fly low, rain comin'," is an old saying. High or low, Swallows are the consummate bug hunters of bird realm. Twittering excitedly from a wire or ledge, these forktailed aerial acrobats launch, dart, and swoop all day with dizzying speed after mosquitoes and other insects to feed themselves and their nestlings. The buffy breasts and orange chins of Barn Swallows distinguish them from the white-bellied Tree and Bank Swallows. Tree Swallows are the earliest to arrive in spring. In southern New England (rarely New Brunswick), the Rough-winged Swallow breeds.

The larger Purple Martin migrates through Atlantic Canada, but, although bird-lovers erect elaborate houses, these handsome birds seldom nest. Even in southern New England, it is common only at local nesting sites.

Although the Cedar Waxwing also catches insects on the wing, its broad hooked bill pro-

Facing page: *Waxwings are tidy, crested birds named for the red waxlike appendages on the tips of their wing feathers. The Cedar Waxwing is a sparrow-sized, year-round resident in New England and southern Nova Scotia and New Brunswick.*

Below: *From a favourite perch, a Belted Kingfisher surveys a stream for minnows and other small fish that it takes by diving. Kingfishers usually nest in stream bank cavities that they excavate with their strong, spear-shaped beaks. When disturbed they utter a harsh, rattling cry and fly off to another perch.*

claims a diet of fruit and berries. Its second name comes from tiny red appendages that look like dots of sealing wax on the tips of its smaller wing feathers.

OTHER BIRDS

THERE IS SOMETHING PLEASANT ABOUT WAKING to the rapid *rat-a-tat-a-tat* of a woodpecker drilling industriously in a tree outside one's window. Between hammer bursts it listens intently for the scurry of startled tenants inside the wood. Woodpeckers belong to the Order *Piciformes* and are highly specialized for mining the trunks and branches of dying trees for wood-boring insects and their larvae. To brace their bodies while clinging to vertical surfaces, their tails are stiff and short, and most species have two of their four toes facing back. They can drill into solid wood because their beaks are straight, chisel-shaped, and sharp. To absorb the impact of repeated hammering, the skull is much thicker and heavier than in other birds. Most unusual of all, coiled within the skull is a long tongue able to probe more than five centimetres into a tree to extract insects on its barbed tip.

Our two most familiar species are the Downy Woodpecker and its larger look alike, the Hairy Woodpecker. They have trans-Canadian ranges in boreal and mixed forests, with the Downy generally operating in smaller trees. Both these forest dwellers show up in urban areas in winter.

Another common member, the Northern Flicker, feeds on the ground more than other Woodpeckers, and has been known to eat five thousand ants in one meal. A wary bird, it is easily recognized at some distance by the rapidly repeated loud cry that gives it its name. Closer it is iden-

tified by its distinctive red crown, white rump patch, and yellow-shafted wings.

Other members of the group are the Yellow-bellied Sapsucker, two Three-toed species, and the rare, crow-sized Pileated Woodpecker. The latter sports a bright red crest and in flight shows a conspicuous white rump patch like the Flicker's; its call is similar too. For nesting the Pileated requires a standing, dead or dying tree at least thirty-six centimetres in diameter. The breeding range of two, the Red-headed and Red-bellied woodpeckers of southern New England, does not extend into Atlantic Canada.

The Belted Kingfisher is unmistakable in looks, voice, and manner. The genteel image of white vest and collar is offset by a shaggy, bluish crest, oversize bill, harsh rattling cry, and its habit of diving from perches along lake shores and stream banks for fish. Although it takes a few small trout and young salmon, parr, minnows, and coarse fish are its main fare. Kingfishers excavate nest tunnels over a metre deep in a vertical bank of sand or compacted sawdust. Both parents feed the young at the entrance.

Cuckoos and Doves have interesting stories. Old World Cuckoos lay their eggs in other birds' nests and leave the risky business of raising young to unwitting foster parents. The similar Black-billed and Yellow-billed cuckoos, our only northern representatives, have better manners. They rear their own young and, in the process, devour vast numbers of caterpillars.

Everyone knows the strutting, cooing pigeon of our cities and grain depots. It is a cruel irony that this mongrel Old World Rock Dove should abound, when its famous New World cousin is extinct. In the stark words of Robie Tufts, "The last Passenger Pigeon died in captivity in a

Left: *A male Downy Woodpecker investigates the dead branch of a white birch for the insects that are its staple food. Like other woodpeckers it has a coiled barb-tipped tongue that it pokes into holes made by its chisel-shaped beak to extract the grubs of wood-boring larvae. This is the smallest of our several species, all of which nest in dead and dying trees.*

Facing Page: *Although it can perch like any other bird, the tiny Ruby-throated Hummingbird more often hovers on blurred wings while it sucks sweet nectar from flowers. It is the only bird that can fly backward and sideways.*

Cincinnati zoo on 1 September 1914." Decades before that, its teeming autumn hordes had been brought low by market hunting and destruction of deciduous forests. Yet, bird-lovers can still catch its likeness in the native Mourning Dove, its smaller long-tailed relative. A common winter resident of Massachusetts, Connecticut, and Rhode Island, it feeds on weed seeds and grain. Sometimes it graces winter feeders in southern New Brunswick and central Nova Scotia with its slender brown presence. In flight it cries a mournful *O-woe-woe-woe*.

The Chimney Swift is a daytime insect hunter that winters in Peru and belongs to the same order as the Hummingbird, the *Alpodiformes.* Swifts spend most of their waking life airborne, even drinking while in flight. They roost clinging to hidden vertical surfaces such as rock clefts, bracing themselves with spiny tail feathers. One chimney in Wolfville, Nova Scotia that shelters hundreds has become a tourist attraction. Swifts are rare in the Maritimes, but common in New England.

Our only Hummingbird is the Ruby-throated. Hovering on blurred wings, it inserts its long curved bill and sips nectar from deep-throated flowers like delphinium and hollyhock, but will also come readily to porch feeders containing sugared water. The female builds a nest about the size of half a walnut shell. Composed of plant down and camouflaged with bits of gray lichen, it is often held in place by a spider's web. Her two offspring are about the size of bumblebees. The male long gone, she defends them fiercely, often chasing other birds away.

The Common Nighthawk is usually more heard than seen. Hawking high for insects, it frequently utters its raspy *scaipe.* At mating time the male creates sonic booms by steep dives and sudden pull outs. Although the bird's bent wings resemble a falcon's, the wide, whiskered beak, held agape to scoop up insects, quickly identify it. Females commonly lay their eggs unprotected on gravel or burnt ground and flat pebbled rooftops. When approached they will feign injury to lure an intruder away from the eggs. Unlike other birds, Nighthawks perch lengthwise to a branch or wire. The song of its small cousin, the Whip-poor-will, is sweet and unmistakable, but even fewer people have seen this nocturnal insect hunter.

SHOREBIRDS AND ALLIES

BETWEEN DRY LAND AND OPEN WATER LIES A food-rich transition zone that shifts with moon and tide. The price of admission is a longish beak for probing wet mud or sand, tall thin legs that offer little resistance to waves, and colours that blend with mossy bog or sandy beach.

For many, the winnowing tremolo of the male Snipe, heard high overhead on a moist May evening, is as much a part of spring as the robin's song. It's only the sound of air whistling through his wing and tail feathers, but it has a heady quality of wildness and promise. Snipe and Woodcock are members of the large and diverse *Scolopacidae* or Sandpiper family, which contains some eighty-eight species worldwide and is represented in the Northeast by two dozen species that breed or pass through. These range in size from the diminutive Least Sandpiper to the Willet Whimbrel, and the Greater Yellowlegs that stand more than thirty centimetres tall. Most are slender, brown and white, highly mobile birds that consort in large flocks and head south in the fall. They have a steady, horizontal gait that makes the smaller members look as if they run on wheels.

Unlike the Plovers that feed by sight, sandpipers have smallish eyes and depend instead on long sensitive bills to locate the burrowing invertebrates that form the bulk of their food. However, the Woodcock's eyes are large and set high on its head, a safety precaution for hunting earthworms in dim woodland thickets. Hunters prize Snipe and Woodcock because they flush from cover explosively, and the Snipe's zigzag flight makes a difficult target. Like the Plover the latter tries to lure predators away from the nest by feigning injury.

Our other common breeding Sandpipers include the Spotted, Solitary, Least (often called "Beachy Bird"), and the Semipalmated; the two largest are the Greater Yellowlegs (most common in Newfoundland and Cape Breton Island) and the Willet. Among the common transients are the Lesser Yellowlegs, Short-billed Dowitcher (Long Island for "Deutcher" to distinguish it from "English" or Common Snipe), Dunlin, and Purple Sandpiper. The latter breeds in the high Arctic and winters on rocky headlands here.

Like the Sandpiper family, the Plover and related Phalaropes are superbly adapted to life in the intertidal zone. Sandpipers and plovers patrol the

Below: *Camouflage colouration and a long bill for probing mud for worms and other delicacies equip the Common Snipe for its role as a land-dwelling sandpiper. It is the mating male of this species that produces the lovely winnowing sound on spring evenings throughout the Northeast.*

Facing page: *The Lesser Yellowlegs is a robin-sized version of the Greater Yellowlegs, both of which are common transients here. Though the latter is breeds in northwestern Canada, they sometimes migrate south together to their wintering areas around the Caribbean, Gulf of Mexico, and South America.*

Below: *Named for one of its cries, this handsome, noisy Killdeer is one of the first to arrive in the spring. For breeding it prefers open ground with sparse grass such as pastures, golf courses, and plowed land. It feeds around lakes, ditches, and moist ground.*

shore on foot, while Phalaropes swim with half-webbed feet and spend much of their lives on the open sea. They are unusual too in that the female does the courting and the male looks after the eggs.

Around July every summer a *whoosh* of wings overhead signals the arrival of the Semipalmated Sandpipers. In tight formation hundreds of small birds whiz by, flash buff and white in the sun, bank as one, and suddenly disappear, only to reappear farther on and fall like autumn leaves onto fields near the Fundy mud flats. The whole performance takes only minutes. Resting until tidefall, they move to the flats, where they dart and probe for small invertebrates and molluscs until sated. They are fattening up for the long flight south to the Caribbean and South American mudflats that they left the previous spring.

Sometimes mingled with them is their paler relative, the endangered Piping Plover. Both breed sparingly here. Typically, the Piping Plover lays its four creamy white eggs in a mere scrape in the sand high above tidewater, trusting camouflage and privacy to protect them. But human intrusion knows no bounds. Nesting and habitat losses in recent years have reduced its numbers alarmingly. There is also the frightful possibility that a super-tanker spill in the lower Bay of Fundy while they are massing for migration could wipe out most of the breeding population. Various agencies are campaigning for this bird's survival.

Our third breeding representative is Killdeer, well-known for the clear, repeated cry that gives it its name, and decidedly Kestrel-like on the wing. Two other species, the Lesser Golden and Black-bellied Plovers, traverse the Northeast on their journeys to and from the high Arctic, but do not breed here. The Upland Plover, called Upland Sandpiper in New England, breeds sparsely in northeastern Maine.

The Eskimo Curlew, a Dowitcher-like shore-bird with a long upturned beak, was once a common transient in the Northeast, flying more than four thousand kilometres non-stop from the Arctic to South America. Unfortunately, uncontrolled hunting may have doomed it to extinction. Although the last recorded specimen was taken at Battle Harbour, Labrador on 29 August 1932, rare sightings raise hopes that it may yet recover.

WATER BIRDS

"GOD MUST HAVE BEEN JOKING WHEN HE MADE A duck," it has been said. Certainly a duck waddling on land is awkward. So is a loon or an auk. Compared with the nimble legs of a barnyard hen, their legs are placed too far back and too far apart for easy walking. Yet, in the water they are all grace and even in the air they are impressive. Ducks and Geese comprise some 150 species worldwide, of which about 30 occur regularly here. For convenience they are classed as dabblers or puddle ducks (those that feed by upending in shallow marshes and ponds) and divers (those that inhabit deeper waters, both salt and fresh).

All water birds feed on aquatic plants or animals and have lobed or webbed toes and strongly muscled legs that propel them easily. Deep divers like the Loon and Cormorant even swim with their wings in pursuit of fish. Lacking sharp talons to grab and hold prey, water birds like Herons and Gannets employ daggerlike beaks. Ducks and Geese, most of which feed on soft plant and animal materials, have broad rubbery beaks suitable for grubbing and sifting.

Except for a few families, all are strong fliers and some ocean species virtually live their whole lives aloft. Water birds occupy habitats as diverse as reedy freshwater marshes, lofty wave-pounded sea cliffs, and the open ocean. In general saltwater species lack the colourful breeding plumage of their freshwater counterparts. Most species merely visit us in going or coming, but about twenty breed here, and a number overwinter from breeding sites farther north.

FRESHWATER BIRDS

When we think of freshwater birds, we are apt to envision ducks paddling in the rain or high honking southbound wedges of Canada Geese that signal winter's onset. And perhaps because ducks and geese are so plentiful and obvious, they overshadow more solitary species like the colourful Grebes, the chickenlike Rails, Coots, and Sora, and the cranelike Herons. This is unfortunate. These interesting birds have their own ingenious adaptations for prospering in the freshwater world. The best known representative is the Common Loon, which has deservedly become a media icon for wilderness.

The term "freshwater bird" should not be taken too literally. Although most spend their lives around ponds, streams, and marshes, some, for instance Geese and Herons, also frequent saltwater habitat such as shallow coastal bays and inlets.

The recipe for a good loon habitat starts with at least a hectare of undisturbed lake offering steady water levels and a minimum of 150 metres of takeoff space. It must have a good supply of fish, frogs, leeches, and insects, an islet for nesting, and a cove for rearing the two dusky chicks. As soon as the ice melts, the Common Loon returns to such lakes, year after year, from our coastal waters. Unfortunately, it often finds the place too noisy and too dirty because of boaters, cottagers, and acid precipitation.

This "Great Northern Diver" catches fish for a living. Although it is as big as a Canada Goose, in flight, its shorter downturned neck and its trailing legs readily identify it. On land it can barely walk, and even on water it requires a long, strenuous, upwind run to get airborne. But it can dive fast enough to escape gunfire, descend to about two hundred metres, and stay underwater for up to

Facing page: *Symbol of wilderness, the Common Loon breeds on undisturbed lakes across southern Canada, where it utters a variety of calls, the most familiar of which is a wild, yodelling laughter. A superb swimmer and diver, it lives on fish that it catches underwater.*

Facing page: *Grebes are small freshwater birds with spoon-shaped toes. They build floating nests of marsh vegetation. The Pied-billed Grebe is the only of five North American species that breeds here. The Horned Grebe, a regular transient, has chestnut flanks and a yellow-crested, jet black head.*

Below: *The ducklike appearance of the American Coot or Mud Hen, a member of the Rail family, shows how similar environments can mould similar forms from entirely different families. The Coot has lobed feet like the Grebe and is awkward on land. Here a female feeds her young.*

three minutes. It can also submerge slowly with hardly a ripple. Throughout its haunts across southern Canada, a wilderness lake without its thrilling tremolo and wolflike *ah-loo* seems unworthy of the name.

The Red-throated Loon, much smaller with an uptilted beak and rusty throat patch, breeds in the far North and is seen here in the Northeast only as a transient.

Grebes, of which only the Pied-billed breeds in the Northeast, somewhat resemble loons, but their toes are lobed not webbed, their bodies are smaller, and their necks are shorter. And they are more sociable. But as swimmers and divers they have the same skills (hence they are sometimes called "Hell-divers"), and like loons they piggyback their young. Unlike loons, which nest on shore, the Pied-bill builds a floating nest in open freshwater marshes. At the Sackville Waterfowl Park in New Brunswick, Pied-billed Grebes are nearly tame and in late summer can be studied at leisure as they raise their young.

Rails, Coots, and Soras belong to the *Rallidae*, a family of marsh skulkers and swimmers that has mastered the disappearing act. "As thin as a rail" refers to its vertically flattened body, an adaptation for marsh living. When approached, rails slip away on delicate feet into the nearest tangle of reeds. Good swimmers and divers, they fly only as a last resort, and then only for a short distance. If closely pursued, they will dive and freeze with only the tip of the bill above water.

Our most common representatives are the plump little brown and gray Sora that breeds in fresh and brackish marshes throughout New England and the Maritimes, and the somewhat larger, very secretive Virginia Rail. They feed chiefly on molluscs, small invertebrates, and plants. The American Coot, a ducklike swimming bird with colourful breeding plumage and a white bill, breeds sparsely on the Tantramar marshes between New Brunswick and Nova Scotia, in southern Maine, and in Massachusetts, lingering past freeze-up. Like the Grebe it builds a floating nest of marsh vegetation. The expression "Clumsy as a coot" comes from its awkwardness on land. It feeds on various invertebrates, seeds, bulbs, and the like. The King and Yellow rail are much rarer in the Maritimes; all are rare or accidental in Newfoundland.

Bitterns belong to the *Ardeidae*, a mainly tropical family of long-billed, long-legged, wading

Facing page: *In preparation for takeoff, a Great Blue Heron treads water to get up speed. It often stands motionless in shallow water with its dagger-like beak poised until a small fish, frog, or snake swim close enough to spear.*

Below: *Like a painted figure carved in wood, the small Green Heron stalks the shore in search of min-nows and frogs.*

birds with broad wings and short tails. The family embraces the Herons and Egrets and is allied to the Stork, Flamingo, and Ibis groups. In the Northeast its most spectacular member is the 130 centimetre-tall Great Blue Heron, whose ability to stand motionless as it fishes around shallow bays and mud flats is legendary. Like the Bittern it grabs or spears its prey with a daggerlike beak, then gulps it down. Fish, frogs, salamanders, insects, snakes, and mice are all grist for its mill. Larger prey is first killed by violent shaking or by

stunning it against a rock or tree. While Bitterns nest on a low platform amid reeds or cattails, Great Blue Herons form rookeries in the tops of conifers on secluded islands or in woods near water.

Lacking an oil gland, the Heron grooms itself with its middle toenail using a chalky powder that it gets from special feathers with its beak.

Bitterns and Herons nest widely across southern Canada and most of the United States, but the latter are absent from Newfoundland. Other relatives that breed sparsely in the Maritimes (except in Prince Edward Island) are the Least Bittern and the Green-backed Heron, and the Black-crowned Night-Heron. The latter two are locally common in New England, as is the Glossy Ibis along the coast from southern Maine to Florida. Vagrants include several other southern Herons and Egrets, some of which are extending their range into New England and the Maritimes.

In colonial times the skies from Long Island Sound to the marshlands of Tantramar and on to Grand Pré and Malpeque and Grand Codroy darkened every spring and fall with clangourous phalanxes of migrating geese and ducks, members of the Anseriformes Order, which also includes swans. Starting with the Acadian farmers of the seventeenth century in the Bay of Fundy, the many marshlands were dyked and drained for agriculture until only a remnant was left. For many decades, until regulations were made and enforced, relentless hunting took its toll. Today agencies like Ducks Unlimited and the Canadian Wildlife Service are slowly reclaiming lost habitat and rebuilding waterfowl populations. Of the many species of Geese and Ducks that migrate through the region, about twenty remain to breed. And the New Brunswick-Nova Scotia border

Left: *Canada Geese mate for life. The gander guards the nest while his mate incubates their four to six white eggs for about twenty-five days. The nest is made of grass and twigs and lined with fluffy down from the female's breast.*

Facing Page: *The Mallard is found worldwide and is the source of most domestic duck strains. In Canada it is most common in the west, but has recently been ranging eastward, where it interbreeds with the Black Duck. Here a female soaks up the morning sun.*

Facing page: *This male Wood Duck in breeding plumage bobs its head with each foot stroke. The crest and white head stripes are unmistakable. When startled the female squeals* cr-r-e-ek, cr-r-e-ek, cr-e-e-ek. *In Nova Scotia and New Brunswick this medium-sized waterfowl is often called a Tree Duck from its habit of perching in trees and nesting in tree cavities.*

remains one of the best spots in Canada for observing diverse waterfowl. Nest-building, incubation, and raising of young are left to the female, which lays three to twelve eggs that take about a month to hatch.

Apart from the white Mute Swan from Europe, which has escaped from captivity and exists in wild or semi-wild colonies chiefly around Long Island Sound, the largest wild representative is the one-metre-long Canada Goose. It is a continental species inhabiting an array of wetlands from treeless northern tundra to southern cypress bayous. Our only breeding goose, it winters from southern Canada, including Atlantic Canada, to the Gulf of Mexico. The birds mate for life and guard their four to six young fiercely. They eat a wide variety of water plants, berries, and grain. Snow Geese and Brant are sometimes seen; the former is a rare newcomer, the latter a coastal migrant.

Most dabblers or puddle ducks sport iridescent wing patches. One of our best known species is the American Black Duck. Other familiar species are the showy Green-winged and Blue-winged Teals and the Northern Pintail. A colourful western Duck that is becoming more common here is the familiar Mallard. It has a circum-polar range and furnishes the breeding stock for many similar domestic strains. Its influx may be causing the current decline in numbers of the closely related native Black Duck, with which it interbreeds.

While both Black and Mallard ducks sometimes nest in trees or even in abandoned hawk nests, the smaller Wood Duck is a true cavity nester. It breeds sparingly through New England and the Maritimes, and the male is considered one of the most beautiful of all Ducks. Wood Ducks exemplify the exacting habitat requirements of some wild birds. They need a hollow

tree at least forty centimetres in diameter with an entrance hole at least ten centimetres across. It must be located in a food-rich area with overhanging foliage for cover, dead snags for perching, and within a few hundred metres of fresh water. The Wood Duck will accept nesting boxes, but the other conditions must be met. It eats land and water insects, acorns (favourite food), waste grains, seeds of aquatic plants, and fleshy fruits.

The nest is built one to twenty metres above ground and some thirty centimetres below the entrance hole. To leave the nest the young, numbering six to fifteen, must first climb up to the hole, then jump out. For the climb, they use their very sharp claws as well as a temporary beak claw. To jump, they spread tiny webbed feet and downy wings that enable them to parachute lightly down. Noted bird breeder Eldon Pace of Shubenacadie, Nova Scotia found that artificially raised chicks need a simulated "landing shock" in order to thrive. Dropping them on the floor was enough.

Severely hunted in the late 1800s for meat and feathers, Wood Ducks have been recovering since the United States and Canada signed the Migratory Birds Treaty in 1916.

Other dabblers sometimes seen are the American Widgeon, Northern Shoveller, and the Gadwall.

Unlike most local diving ducks, which summer in inland waters but winter in coastal areas, the Ring-necked frequents fresh water year-round. It also has the unorthodox habit of swimming far out on wide bodies of water and the puddle duck's ability to spring directly into the air without a takeoff run. The beautiful Harlequin of swift-running streams in the West also winters in small numbers in Newfoundland, New Brunswick, and New England.

Facing page: *A male Red-breasted Merganser parades in breeding plumage with its crest erect. The ideal breeding habitat for this circum- polar, fish-eating duck is a small island in a forest or coastal setting, with low woody growth or long-hanging conifer limbs. It nests on the ground in dense cover. In the Northeast it tends to be more common in winter, especially in sheltered coastal waters.*

Below: *Like the Common and Hooded Merganser, the Common Goldeneye requires a cavity tree for nesting. A diving duck of woodland lakes in nesting season, it winters in Northeastern coastal waters and on rivers where the current is strong enough to maintain open water.*

The Merganser (also called Shelduck in Nova Scotia and New Brunswick, and Gossard in Newfoundland and Labrador) is the only freshwater Duck with a cylindrical, saw-toothed bill, ideal for holding slippery prey. The Common, Hooded, and Red-breasted all breed here; the latter is the most common. All three are crested, strikingly beautiful birds, especially the males in breeding finery. They often mingle with seabirds, but the fishy taste of their meat largely protects them from hunting.

While puddle ducks nest on or near dry land, diving ducks normally build over water.

SALTWATER BIRDS

The ocean with its islands and shorelines, shallows and deeps offers such a vast array of habitat and food that it boasts a corresponding variety of bird life. Its representatives range from delicate little Petrels and Terns to large predators like the Gannet. The best known seabirds are Gulls, those tireless wanderers of the world's coastal shipping lanes. Although our only North Atlantic Penguin, the flightless Great Auk, was extirpated in the 1800s, several smaller flying relatives still flourish in the North Atlantic. Despite enlightened hunting regulations, their future is shadowed by overfishing, pesticide contamination, and oil spills. Others, like the rare and lovely Roseate Tern, are threatened by the upsurge of Herring Gull numbers, largely fuelled by our modern abundance of garbage and fishing waste.

Although the Redhead and Ruddy duck breed sparingly in the Northeast, most bay and sea ducks that we see are divers migrating along our coasts to and from breeding grounds farther north or west. Among these are the Common Goldeneye, three species of Scoter (Black, White-winged, and Surf), and the Greater Scaup or Bluebill. Rare transients include the Lesser Scaup from farther west and the Canvasback heading south through New England. The Oldsquaw in its striking, white-streaked winter plumage is worth mentioning here because its numbers have declined markedly in recent years, and because it somewhat resembles the extinct Labrador Duck. The last recorded specimen of that bird was shot at Elmira, New York on 12 December 1878. Robie Tufts blames egging rather than overhunting for its demise.

Probably, our best known and most abundant sea duck is the Common Eider, which lives along

Facing page: *Most gulls nest on the ground or on cliffs on offshore islands or other undistrubed locations. The Herring Gull is the dominant species in our region for most of the year.*

our coasts all year. These strong, heavily built ducks seem to relish the rough winter seas off our headlands and islands. They nest in colonies on islands, using grass and vegetable debris lined with down from their breasts. In winter hunters endure many hardships to bring home a few meals of these prized sea ducks. The slightly larger King Eider winters off Newfoundland, but sometimes appears in the same flocks.

Gulls and terns are the crows and jays of the sea. Yet, they have not severed all ties to terra firma. Gulls are long-winged swimming birds with webbed feet and slightly hooked beaks. Adults are usually white and gray with black markings; the young are brownish. Gulls have squarish or rounded tails, and usually pick their food off the ground or from the water surface. Terns are mostly smaller with sharper reddish beaks, shorter legs, and distinctly forked tails; they dive for their food. Both are gregarious, noisy birds without which our summer coastline would be unnaturally quiet.

The closely related Jaegers and Skuas are hawk-like hunters and parasites of gulls, terns, and other seabirds, forcing them to drop their catch or vomit up their latest meal, which they then snap up in midair.

Our best known year-round gulls are the

Right: *An adult Common Tern (reddish beak) prepares to resume fishing after feeding its large offspring, which gapes for more. Foraging along our coasts and inland waters, this tern hunts by diving from a height. It breeds widely in eastern North America and for nesting prefers open sandy or gravelly beaches near sparse vegetation.*

Herring and Great Black-backed or Saddle-back. The latter breeds on cliffs and islands in coastal lakes from Cape Chidley in Labrador west to Quebec City and south to Long Island Sound. Its major foods are the eggs and young of other seabirds, carrion, and garbage from dumps.

The slightly smaller Herring Gull has a coast-to-coast distribution and similar scavenging habits, but also flocks to fields or barrens to feed on insects, mice, or berries. It has been observed dropping sea urchins and rock crabs from a height to crack them on the rocks below.

Over a dozen other species frequent the Northeast. Among them are the Ring-billed and Bonaparte's of the summer months and northern visitors such as the Iceland, Glaucous, and Ivory Gull in winter. The Black-headed Gull that appears mostly around wharves and fish plants in Newfoundland and Nova Scotia is a visitor from Europe; a few breed here.

The Common Kittiwake or Tickle-ace, as it is called in Newfoundland, is a bird of the open sea that breeds on coasts and islands along the north shore of the St. Lawrence, on Anticosti Island, and around Newfoundland. Unlike most gulls it makes a neat cup-shaped nest of seaweed and grasses. Good places to see Kittiwakes and other seabirds are on crossings of the Newfoundland, Saint John, and Bar Harbour ferries.

Two gull-like birds that stay farther offshore are the Northern Fulmar, a constant companion when nets are being hauled, and the Shearwater (three species), named for its habit of skimming the waves. The latter breeds in the Southern Hemisphere.

We have five breeding species of terns, of which the most abundant are the Common and Arctic. Their sharp clear cry, *stearin, stearin*, gives them their usual name in Newfoundland. Their nervous, bounding flight is tireless. Unlike most gulls, terns migrate south for the winter. The Arctic Tern does so by a roundabout way, crossing the Atlantic to Africa and travelling from there to the waters off South Africa and Antarctica. According to Earl Godfrey, a bird banded in Labrador in late July 1928 was retaken in Natal, South Africa that November.

The goose-sized Northern Gannet is a member of the Booby family and the largest of our seabirds. A white bird with black-tipped wings, it fishes by plunging headlong, wings folded, from heights of up to thirty metres into the ocean to catch a herring or mackerel that it has spotted far beneath the surface. Gannets breed in large colonies at Bonaventure Island, Gaspé, Funk Island, and Cape St. Mary's, Newfoundland. They lay one large, bluish egg in a seaweed nest close by other nests. Young birds are blackish until their fourth year. That they once bred in Maritime waters is confirmed by two "Gannet Rocks" in the Bay of Fundy and one near Yarmouth. Gannets winter off the Eastern Seaboard from Virginia to the Gulf of Mexico.

Cormorants or Shags are also consummate fish-catchers, but they do not go in for power dives. They chase down their prey under water and grab them in their serrated beaks. (The Chinese use captive cormorants for this purpose. To prevent them from swallowing the catch, they equip each bird with a neck ring. They reward them with a small fish later.) Unlike other seabirds, Cormorants have neither oil glands nor feather dust, so they must dry their plumage often. This explains their habit of standing spread-winged along piers and cliff ledges in the sun. The advantage is that they can eliminate trapped air from

Facing page: *The Northern Gannet congregates in huge breeding colonies. Despite the din and confusion, individual birds manage to find their mates and young. The even engage in affectionate displays amid the hubbub. Gannets are keen-eyed hunters that catch fish by plummeting from a height.*

Facing page: *The colourful, vertically elongated beak of the Puffin gives this small, portly member of the Auk family its nickname of Sea Parrot. The largest Canadian colony of Puffins is at Witless Bay, Newfoundland. Puffins feed mainly on capelin, a member of the smelt family.*

the feathers, thus slimming the body for greater underwater speed and manoeuvrability. Our two species are the resident Great Cormorant and the Double-crested, which is rare here in winter.

The extinct Great Auk, which belonged to the *Alcidae*, was once found as far south as Nova Scotia and on both sides of the North Atlantic. From Cartier's time until the early 1800s, this flightless, near-tame, eighty-centimetre-tall Auk, which laid only one egg a year, was slaughtered for meat, feathers, eggs, and oil. The last one seen alive was on Eldey Rock, Iceland on 3 June 1844.

The living relatives of the Great Auk are the Auks, Murres, and Puffins. These expert swimmers and divers are characterized by short necks and sober, black-and-white plumage. Of the living auks, the small Razor-bill or Tinker with its vertically flattened beak looks most like its vanished ancestor, especially when sitting erect. But it is only half the size, and it can fly. The larger Common Murre and Thick-billed Murre have pointed beaks. Murre (or Turr) gather in large numbers off the Newfoundland and Labrador coasts in winter where many are legally shot by coastal residents, who relish and need the fresh meat. The robin-sized Dovekie or Bull-bird (in reference to its short neck) and Razor-bill are protected by law. Dovekies feed on plankton by swimming underwater with their beaks open like tiny whales.

The Black Guillemot or Pigeon, which turns white in winter, has one of the widest breeding ranges of all our seabirds. It nests among boulders and rock crevices from the Bay of Fundy to the high Arctic. They live on small bottom-living fishes which somehow they ferret out from under boulders and floating seaweed in the dark. Some guillemots stay on through the high Arctic's per-

petual midwinter darkness.

Most people's favourite seabird is the portly Atlantic Puffin or Sea Parrot, which has an over-size vertically elongated beak decorated with red and yellow stripes. Like the Murre and Razorbill, it feeds by "flying" underwater after small fish like the silvery capelin. After wintering far out on the ocean, Puffins move inshore in summer to breed at a few places like Machias Seal Island near Grand Manan, New Brunswick, the Funks, and at Newfoundland's Witless Bay. Like the Great Auk, they lay but one egg in a burrow. The Newfoundland population has declined in recent years; some blame heavy fishing of capelin, their chief food during breeding season.

Like the Puffin, the Leach's Petrel or "Mother Carey's Chicken" lives at sea but comes ashore once a year to breed. A gentle, sooty-black, fork-tailed bird slightly larger than a swallow, it too burrows in the earth. Both sexes take turns incubating the single egg and feeding the chick at night, often going without food for two days until the partner returns. During the day the colony is silent. Wilson's Petrel is a winter visitor from the Southern Hemisphere. Both have white wing and rump patches, but the latter's tail is square. These birds skim tidbits from the sea, and often dabble their feet in it. So they can breathe while skimming, the beak is equipped with breathing tubes on top.

AMPHIBIANS & REPTILES

Facing page: *A Newt is an aquatic salamander that hatches in water, but spends some time on land before returning to its fresh water habitat. On land it forages mostly on snails, springtails, and soil mites during rainy weather. In ater it eats aquatic invertebrates.*

Below: *Frogs and Toads hatch from eggs laid in water and, depending on the species, spend anywhere from a few weeks to three years as fishlike tadpoles before absorbing their tails and becoming true air-breathing amphibians.*

IN THE PARADE OF LIFE, AMPHIBIANS REPRESENT A stage between water and land, while reptiles have made a break. Salamanders, frogs, and toads all require water in which to lay their eggs, and their young go through a fishlike tadpole stage before crawling out on land. Most turtles and snakes, however, have their young on land. Snakes drink water and may hunt in it, but otherwise they live on land. Turtles stay near water, and a few spend the lives in it, but they do not fear dehydration the way a frog or salamander does.

What makes this possible is a watertight skin—something a water dweller doesn't need. A frog or salamander left in the sun too long will die from evaporation and overheating. Turtles and snakes, on the other hand, like nothing better than to sunbathe, provided the temperature is reasonable. The salamander can't even drink; it must absorb water through the skin.

Amphibians and reptiles are cold-blooded. Strictly speaking this is a misnomer, since on a hot day their blood can be quite warm, while a fish's blood stays at the same steady temperature as the surrounding water. Correctly speaking they are ectotherms—creatures whose body temperatures match the outside temperature, be it cold or warm. Unlike birds and mammals, which are endotherms, they have no internal way of regulating body temperature and no external insulation. Heat for them is more dangerous than cold; temperatures above 36°C are fatal. The advantage is that they burn very little energy. This is why snakes can go so long without food, and why frogs and turtles can easily hibernate for six months under the mud in a frozen pond.

Although amphibians can survive on land, they never stray far from water even as adults. Hatching as elongated larvae that breathe through gills, they later develop air sacs or lungs that allow them to breathe out of water. Salamanders migrate overland on rainy, spring nights to special freshwater breeding ponds to mate and lay their eggs. Frogs and toads also mate and lay their eggs in water. Unlike salamanders, they later absorb their tails. Most mature salamanders keep moist by living in damp and dark forest places under vegetation and rotting wood, while frogs and toads inhabit the margins and shallows of freshwater ponds and swamps where they were born.

Salamanders are full of biological surprises. Newts are salamanders that reverse the normal sequence by spending their adult lives in water after a juvenile stage on land.

The large Mudpuppy (up to forty centimetres), found from New England southward, is a wholly aquatic, weak-limbed salamander. Instead of switching to air breathing, the Mudpuppy retains the juvenile's external gills all its life, as does the eel-like southern Mud siren. Whereas all of our species have four legs from birth, the Mud siren lacks hind legs.

Many amphibian populations are declining due to human interference. This includes pollution, acid precipitation, and loss of habitat from logging and the draining and filling of swamps for construction and agriculture.

AMPHIBIANS

SALAMANDERS
Salamanders have a froglike face and a lizard's tail. In fact, their common name comes from Greek word meaning lizard, the name of their Order, *Caudata*, is Latin for tailed. The usual background colour of their heads, backs, and sides is dark to match their habitat. They are decorated

Facing page: *Looking like a gaudy lizard in a wet suit, salamanders are scaleless creatures which, like all amphibians, must stay moist to survive. The Yellow-spotted Salamander inhabits moist woods near aquatic breeding sites. Many embryos of this salamander die if acidity reaches pH 5 or below.*

with colourful dots or blotches to break the body outline and perhaps warn predators. Their bellies are usually plain and grayish. Most adults range from five to fifteen centimetres, depending on the species.

Although few ever see these mysterious little creatures, they are by no means rare. Most are active only at night or in dim light. Three families—the Mole Salamanders, Lungless Salamanders, and Newts—are represented in the Northeast by over a dozen species. About nine occur in the Maritimes and thirteen in New England, but none in Newfoundland. Among these are the Spotted, Redback, Northern Dusky, and Northern Two-lined. The latter two inhabit southern and western New Brunswick, respectively; both are common in New England.

Two of the prettiest are the Yellow-Spotted Salamander, a common species with large canary-yellow blotches on a brownish to blackish background, and the Blue-spotted, which has dusky blue spots on a blue-black background. These are thick-bodied members of the mole or burrowing group, up to fifteen centimetres long. Both occur throughout the Northeast; the latter, with allied forms, is also found along the southern coast of Labrador. Soon after the ice melts they migrate to forest ponds or roadside ditches to mate.

The Four-toed Salamander is a lungless bog species rare in New England and Nova Scotia and absent from New Brunswick, northern Maine, and Prince Edward Island. The most terrestrial is the Eastern Redback. This lungless species, found from the Carolinas to Labrador, lives its entire life in mixed woods, inhabiting the interiors of decaying logs and stumps. It is also found under bark, stones, and moist leaf litter.

Fertilization is normally achieved in spring by

the male depositing a bit of sperm on the ground and the female picking it up with her cloaca and storing it in her body until egg-laying time a little later. Most lay from one hundred to three hundred eggs singly or in a few clumps on underwater vegetation; these take about one month to hatch. Most salamanders live on insects, mites, millipedes, and worms, but some catch mayflies and other insects. In turn they are preyed on by many creatures, including fish, frogs, snakes, herons, and sometimes each other. They hibernate underground or under water.

Our only Newt is the Red-spotted, about ten centimetres long. Newts have rougher skin than that of other salamanders, and their offspring have an elfin name: efts. Adults inhabit unpolluted shallow water of lakes, marshes, ditches, and slow-moving streams, preferably with plenty of submerged vegetation. The 200-375 eggs, which they attach singly to the leaves of aquatic plants, hatch in three to five weeks. Juveniles are fiery red (hence Red Efts). Some stay in the home waters, eat well, and mature in two years; but most live dangerously for up to eight years in the forest before returning to water. These eat only during summer rains. Like all amphibians, newts exude a slimy skin coating with somewhat toxic properties. The Red Eft's toxin is ten times stronger than the adult's.

FROGS AND TOADS

Surely one of the sweetest sounds in Nature is the high-pitched chorus of a Northern Spring Peeper choir on a misty April night. As early as March, these tiny (about three centimetres long) brown or gray frogs climb on vegetation near shallow water to proclaim their love. Should an intruder approach, they abruptly cease. If the

thermometer dips, they may halt. But let the intruder leave or the temperatures rise, and they resume their serenade.

Frogs are tailless, neckless amphibians of the Order *Anura.* They are endowed with webbed hind toes and very specialized hind legs that allow them to swim almost as well as fish and to leap like rabbits. Unlike fish that detect underwater vibrations through their lateral line, amphibians have developed eardrums. Frogs and toads not only hear very well, but possess well-developed vocal chords. Because they have weak lungs, they augment the air supply by inflating their throats. Anyone who has experienced the excruciating din of a full frog symphony nearby knows how effective this can be. Another innovation of frogs and toads is their extendable sticky tongue. Unlike ours, which are attached at the back, theirs are hinged from the front and can be snapped out and back at blinding speed to snare flying insects.

Frogs look wet and toads look dry, but the difference is only skin-deep. In all, the Northeast has about a dozen species of toads (Family *Bufonidae*), treefrogs (*Hylidae*), and true frogs (*Ranidae*). Of these, one toad, two treefrogs, and six true frogs are found in Nova Scotia and New Brunswick.

Left: Although the Eastern Toad is drier to the touch than a frog, it needs constant moisture or it will die. Like the frog it breeds in water, but then spends most of its time on land hunting insects, sowbugs, spiders slugs, and earthworms in the evening hours.

Facing page: The largest of the Northeast's native frogs, a Bullfrog prowls among water weeds in search of almost any small prey: insects, snails, spiders, salamanders, birds, snakes, and other frogs, including its own kind.

Above: *One of North America's most widespread amphibians is the handsome Northern Leopard Frog. During summer it prefers wet open meadows and fields and wet woods. In winter it hibernates under the muddy bottoms of ponds or in damp caves. Its chief food is insects.*

Facing page: *The Wood Frog is found from Alaska to Labrador (but not Newfoundland) and south to Georgia. Though less tied to water than most frogs, it does need ponds for breeding and hibernates in flooded meadows or under moist forest debris.*

Three of the latter also occur in Prince Edward Island. According to John Gilhen, author of the Nova Scotia Museum's *Amphibians and Reptiles of Nova Scotia*, the rare Gray Treefrog is known with certainty from only one locality in New Brunswick. Newfoundland had no native frogs or toads, but since the 1930s the Green Frog has been introduced to ponds on the Avalon and Bonavista peninsulas. The Eastern American Toad was introduced in 1960.

It is easy to mistake a resting Eastern American Toad for a clod of earth or some matted fallen leaves. Toads of this species from different habitats vary in colour from dark brownish to grayish or even black, with whitish bellies. These harmless creatures, which measure 50-105 millimetres long (females are larger), trill melodiously from the shores of ponds and streams in May and June, often blending with the Peepers. They eat enormous quantities of invertebrates, including sowbugs, centipedes, beetles, flies, hornets, earthworms, and slugs. Southern New England has two similar species, namely Fowler's Toad and the rare Eastern Spadefoot. A far northern race, the Hudson's Bay Toad, occurs from the coast of Labrador to James Bay.

Our six true frogs are the Bullfrog, Green, Pickerel, Mink, Northern Leopard, and Wood Frog. Except for the Wood and Pickerel, all are patterned with greenish-brown (sometimes with bluish phases) over the back and head, shading to gray, yellow or creamy white on the belly. In most species, and especially the male Bullfrog, the eardrum or "tympanum" is a conspicuous circle, often of a different colour, behind the bulging eye. Wood Frogs are relatively unspotted and vary in colour from rusty through mauve to dark brown, exactly like that of old fallen leaves in the forest. The Pickerel Frog is patterned with dark browns over buff, shading to yellow underneath. Our largest true frog is the Bullfrog (ten to fifteen centimetres), and the smallest is the Mink Frog (five to seven centimetres).

Habitat requirements of the various species overlap, but in general, they have definite preferences and needs. Bullfrogs like bodies of deep permanent water and are the last to emerge in spring. Wood Frogs need temporary woodland pools and sluggish back waters for breeding. The Pickerel Frog requires cooler waters such as lakes, ponds, sphagnum bogs, and limestone quarry pools. Leopard Frogs are found mostly in wet open

Above: *The Snapping Turtle favours bodies of water with soft muddy banks and bottoms where it ambushes unwary fish, snakes, birds, and mammals. It also eats plant material. Though equipped with a powerful beak, it rarely attacks humans.*

Facing page: *This Eastern Painted Turtle peers cautiously at the camera. One of the most common turtles in the Northeast, it is found from mainland Nova Scotia south to Alabama. This little reptile inhabits quiet shallow ponds, marshes, wet meadows, slow-moving streams, and even salt marshes. It likes to bask in the sun.*

meadows, fields, and wet woods. Mink Frogs inhabit lakes and ponds from Manitoba to Labrador and Anticosti and south to the Great Lakes and northern Maine, favouring inlets where cold streams enter; they especially like plenty of lily pads to sit on. Of our species the Wood and Leopard frogs inhabit the greatest range, occurring across the continent, including Labrador. Next to them in geographical spread are the Bullfrog and Green frog, both of which frequent most of eastern North America.

In their vast numbers these interesting creatures devour untold millions of flies and mosquitoes, and, in turn, provide food for a wide range of water creatures.

Reptiles

WHEN WE THINK OF REPTILES MOST OF US imagine snakes. But lizards, crocodiles, tuatara, and turtles are reptiles too. So were the dinosaurs. Reptiles are back-boned animals that have scales, usually lay shelled eggs, and depend on outside sources for their body heat. Because of this, the five families that make up this group reach their greatest diversity in tropical regions. The only reptiles native to the Northeast are snakes and turtles. Except the Timber Rattlesnake, whose range extends into southern New England, none of these is poisonous, and only one, the Snapping Turtle, has a dangerous bite. Contrary to popular belief, the skin of snakes, unlike that of amphibians, is clean, dry, and silky to the touch. Snakes shed their scaly skins completely—even the eye coverings—as they grow larger. In earlier societies this habit led to a belief that these creatures could die and come to life again. Turtles, on the other hand, were commonly thought to live forever.

The skink looks like a salamander but has scales like the lizard that it is; only one species, the Five-lined (about 15 centimetres long), occurs in our region, in western Connecticut.

FRESHWATER TURTLES

Turtles are reptiles that live in tough keratin boxes. It is the safest way to live, since nothing can get at them. But the price is high. They have to lug a heavy load of fused scales everywhere they go. This slows them down considerably. It also makes breathing difficult. Since they don't have a rib cage, they must suck in with their flank muscles and push out with other muscles to keep the air moving. On the plus side, they can pull their snakelike heads completely into the space formed by the top and bottom shells, curving the long neck into an S to do so. After a careful stalk and a prolonged wait, a quick dart of the head can capture a meal. While turtles lack teeth, they manage to tear prey with a sharp-edged, birdlike beak.

Turtles grow very slowly. Larger forms such as the sea turtle may live a century or more; smaller ones are thought to have life spans measured in decades. Like amphibians, they spend the winter in a deep sleep at the muddy bottom of a pond or other body of water.

Turtles lay white leathery eggs in nests that they dig or scrape in various materials. The eggs are covered and left in the warm sun to fate. Most predation is at this stage. Bears, raccoons, and crows are known to rob turtle nests. Yet, the survival of the small number of eggs laid by various species suggests that the method is adequate for normal demands.

Land turtles are sometimes called tortoises and water turtles terrapins, but properly speaking both are turtles. The best known species found in west-

Facing page: *The Garter Snake, which grows up to ninety centimetre and comes in various colour phases, is one of best known of the Maritimes' five native snakes. It preys on toads, frogs, mice, other snakes, and a variety of invertebrates. The Garter Snake bears live young and is an excellent swimmer.*

Below: *The Red-Bellied Turtle is found only from Cape Hatteras north to New York, with an isolated population in ponds and coves in Plymouth County, Massachusetts. Listed as endangered in the United States, it feeds mainly on aquatic vegetation, especially milfoil and bladderwort.*

ern Nova Scotia and the lower half of New Brunswick are the Eastern Painted, Wood, and Snapping turtles. Of these, the Snapping Turtle has the broadest range, being found across southern Canada from the Rockies to the Atlantic and south to the Gulf states. An isolated population of Blanding's Turtle inhabits vegetated coves and bogs of Kejimkujik Lake and western Grafton Lake in southwestern Nova Scotia; other isolated populations of this species occur in southern Ontario, Quebec, New York, New Hampshire, eastern Massachusetts, Minnesota, and Pennsylvania. Its shell is a dark, dappled, bluish gray.

The little Eastern Painted Turtle (with a top shell about fifteen centimetres long) and its southern cousins, decorated with yellow lines and red hieroglyphics on a dark, greenish background, are favourites with pet store operators. These little reptiles live on aquatic insects, snails, and minnows. The female lays two to eleven eggs in a nest dug near the shore of a quiet, shallow pond. Normally the hatchlings emerge in late fall and head for water, but if the temperatures are too cool they will hibernate in the nest until spring.

The Common Wood or "Mud" Turtle has a brownish carapace (top shell) sixteen to twenty centimetres long, distinctively ridged with pyramidal plates roughened by steplike markings. The head and neck are dark gray above and rusty below, and the plastron (lower shell) is black with a dull yellow grid. Wood Turtles live along slow, meandering streams with sand or gravel banks for nesting. They travel up feeder streams foraging on horsetails, berries, earthworms, slugs, and insects. Like Painted Turtles, they often bask for a few hours in the afternoon sun. In late June or early July the adult female digs a hole and lays four to

twelve ellipsoidal eggs. Hatchlings emerge in the fall and hibernate in the stream bottom. Like the adults, they lie with heads withdrawn, their bodies wedged against submerged anchored stumps and logs where the current is slack.

With its bulldog neck, spiky forelegs, bony crested tail, and pugnacious jaw, the large (twenty-three to thirty-three centimetres) Common Snapping Turtle looks more primitive than other species, and it is. But its reputation for aggressiveness is overblown. Since it is an aquatic species and often lurks under water in lakes and ponds, swimmers worry that it will attack. Actually, it is quite shy around humans and will move away from a swimmer. If accosted, however, it will lunge and try to bite. The wide, strong jaws can inflict a nasty wound. Normally, they use them on fish, amphibians, and aquatic invertebrates. Snapping Turtles also take some birds, reptiles, and small mammals. Prey is located by sight and a sharp sense of smell, and devoured under water.

In May the female lays around thirty eggs in a nest dug in sand, gravel, sawdust, or soil, not necessarily near water. Females near their nests are especially hostile. The hatchlings emerge around October and hibernate.

Two species absent from Atlantic Canada but common in New England are the Midland Painted and Eastern Box turtles. Uncommon species include the Map Turtle, Red-eared Slider, Eastern Spiny Softshell, and Spotted Turtle. Two species, the Bog and Plymouth Redbelly turtles, are endangered.

SALTWATER TURTLES
Three marine Turtles, namely the small Atlantic Ridley, the larger Atlantic Loggerhead, and the Atlantic Leatherback, visit New England

Facing page: Fond of grass and heath vegetation, the little Northern Red-bellied Snake is a boon to gardeners and blueberry growers because it feeds entirely on slugs.

and Canadian waters every summer. Often they become entangled in fishing nets. The latter two commonly weigh up to 150 kilograms and 545 kilograms, respectively, with the Loggerhead exceeding 175 centimetres in length. All three have short necks and elongated flipperlike forelegs. They lack the claws found on all land turtles. The Leatherback is further adapted for ocean life by streamlined fore-and-aft ridges on its carapace, and by its whalelike colouration—gray above and mottled white beneath.

Due to extensive market hunting for skins and shells, and egg collection for human consumption in the South, all three species are considered endangered.

SNAKES

At first glance snakes seem to lack a lot of basic equipment, but they compensate in other ways. Unlike turtles and most amphibians, they are legless. All snakes move by wavelike muscular contractions that hitch their wide, shinglelike, belly scales forward and back. As these catch on the roughness of the ground, the snake moves forward. On the final approach to prey, this allows it to move without telltale lateral movement. Also, they have no eardrums or vocal chords. The only way they can hear is through vibrations which the skull bones pick up from the ground. But their sense of smell, delivered through the forked tongue that constantly flickers in and out, is acute. And snakes have no eyelids. Instead the eyes are protected by a glassy covering through which they stare unblinking. This, as much as the risk of being bitten, probably contributes to the fear many people have of these creatures.

Snakes are very successful predators that have been on earth for some 300 million years and

show every sign of persisting. In temperate latitudes they hibernate in the ground from autumn through spring. Though perhaps not particularly intelligent— their brains are small and resemble those of birds—their instincts are highly evolved and perfectly attuned to the ecosystems they inhabit. Most of them are also beautifully coloured to match those surroundings. Despite the many myths spun about them—that they sting with their tongues, milk cows, roll tail-in-mouth like a hoop, or swallow their young to protect them—snakes are among the most interesting and beneficial creatures on earth.

Our five Maritime species are all toothed land snakes, however, none is venomous nor can they inflict a serious wound. They range in length from the smallest, the Northern Redbelly (about twenty to thirty centimetres) to the Garter Snake (about forty to ninety centimetres). Between these in approximate ascending order are the Ringnecked, Eastern Smooth Green, and Northern Ribbon snakes.

The Garter and Green snakes are found throughout the Maritimes, including Cape Breton Island and Prince Edward Island, but are absent from insular Newfoundland; Garter Snakes occur along the south shore of Labrador. Ringnecks are generally confined to western Nova Scotia and southern New Brunswick. All but the Maritime Garter and Ribbon Snakes are common in most of New England, which also has seven other common species not found in the Maritimes, and two that are uncommon or rare there.

Snake identification can be confusing since even in one species there can be several variants. Thus, the Redbelly has gray, blue, and brown types, all with red underparts, and the Maritime Garter Snake comes in a striped and unstriped brown model and an all-black version sometimes mistaken for the big Northern Black Racer in New England. However, the Ribbon Snake's pattern of triple yellow dorsal stripes divided by blue lines is dependable. Likewise the Northern Ringneck's grayish back and orange belly and collar is easy to recognize. The little Green Snake's simple grass green garment is easiest of all to identify.

The Green Snake lives in upland grassy or shrubby openings or near bogs and ponds. When alarmed, it is as likely to climb a bush as it is to hide in the vegetation. Its usual food consists of moth larvae, spiders, grasshoppers, and small snails. The Ringneck prefers woodlands and is largely nocturnal. It preys chiefly on the Red-back Salamander and baby snakes. Garter Snakes inhabit a wide variety of habitats from forest to cropland and lakeshore. They occur in most of North America south of James Bay and east of the Coastal Range. They swim readily and are large enough to take frogs and toads as well as salamanders. They are also an important predator of Meadow Voles. The Ribbon Snake is even more partial to water, hunting in shallow ponds for frogs and newts. The Redbelly inhabits upland woody ridges, moist woods, and is often found near the foundations of abandoned buildings. It burrows under surface debris and lives almost entirely on slugs.

Snakes mate in the spring after hibernation, and, in some cases, in the fall. Fertilization is internal by means of an organ near the base of the male's tail that can be everted to enter the cloaca of the female. Two of our native species lay eggs and three bear their young live. Typical egg-laying places are in rotten logs or under stones (one to eight eggs, Northern Ringneck) and under rocks or decaying wood in sunny places (three to eight eggs, Green Snake). Eggs are generally laid in mid-to late summer, and hatch in late summer to early autumn. Females of the Garter, Ribbon, and Redbelly snakes give birth to live young. In Nova Scotia, the estimated numbers are six to forty for Garter snakes, six to ten for the Ribbon Snakes, and three to twelve for the Redbelly.

The two poisonous snakes in New England are the Timber Rattlesnake (except Maine and Rhode Island) and the Northern Copperhead (in Connecticut and a bit of southern Massachusetts). Uncommon to rare this far north, these large reptiles prefer open woodland with rocky slopes with access to water in summer. Their young are born alive. The other seven native snakes range in size from the Black Rat Snake (often 180 centimetres) down to the Eastern Worm and the Northern Brown (as small as 18 and 23 centimetres, respectively). The others are the Eastern Milk, Northern Black Racer, Eastern Hognosed, and Northern Water. The latter prefers slow-running or still water and more than half of its diet consists of fish. The others eat a variety of small mammals, amphibians, birds and their eggs, as well as insects and slugs.

The Hognosed Snake has a small nose flap for burrowing. It feigns death by rolling belly-up when threatened. And it plays the part so well that, when turned right side up, it may roll back over!

SOURCES

Amphibians and Reptiles of Nova Scotia. John Gilhen. N.S. Museum, Halifax, 1984.

The Birds of Canada. W. Earl Godfrey. National Museum of Canada, Bull. No. 203, Biological Series No. 73, Ottawa, 1966.

The Birds of Newfoundland. Harold S. Peters, Thomas D. Burley. Department of Natural Resources, St. Johns, 1951.

The Birds of Nova Scotia. Robie W. Tufts. N.S. Museum/Nimbus Publishing Ltd., Halifax, 1986.

Canadian Mammals. Austin W. Cameron. National Museum of Canada, Ottawa, 1966.

Familiar Wildlife of PEI. P.E.I. Department of the Environment, Charlottetown, [no date].

The Fascination of Reptiles. Maurice Richardson. Hill and Wong, New York, 1972.

A Field Guide to the Birds. Roger Tory Peterson. Houghton Mifflin Co., Boston, 1947.

A Field Guide to Reptiles and Amphibians. Roger Conant. Houghton Mifflin Co., Boston, 1958.

Folk Names of Canadian Birds. W.L. Atree. Bull. No. 149, Biological Series No. 51. National Museum of Canada, Ottawa, 1957.

The Grand Design. Sally Foy/Oxford Scientific Films. Prentice-Hall, Englewood Cliffs, N.J., 1982.

Guide to the Seabirds of Eastern Canada. A.J. Gaston. Environment Canada, Ottawa, 1984.

The Habitat Guide to Birding. Thomas P. McElroy, Jr., Alfred A Knopf, New York, 1974.

Hinterland Who's Who. Canadian Wildlife Service, Environment Canada, Ottawa, (various dates).

Jacques Cousteau: Whales (trans. I. M. Paris). H.N. Abrams, New York, 1988.

Life on Earth. David Attenborough. Little, Brown and Company, Toronto, 1979.

Mammals of North America, Victor Cahalane. MacMillan Company, New York, 1961.

The Natural History of Mammals. François Boulière (trans. H.M. Parshley). Alfred A. Knopf, New York, 1970.

New England Wildlife: Habitat, Natural History, and Distribution. Richard M. De Graaf, Deborah D. Rudis. General Technical Report NE-108, U.S. Department of Agriculture, Forest Service, Washington, D.C., 1983.

Notes on Nova Scotia Wildlife. N.S. Department of Lands and Forests, Halifax, 1978.

Pictorial Guide to the Birds of North America. Leonard Lee Rue III. Thomas W. Crowell, New York, 1970.

Pictorial Guide to the Mammals of North America. Leonard Lee Rue III. Thomas W. Crowell, New York, 1967.

The Reptiles. Life Nature Library. Time/Life Books, New York, 1963.

The Seals of Nova Scotia Waters. Frederick Scott. N.S. Museum/Journal of Education, Halifax, 1968.

The Year of the Whale. Victor B. Scheffer. Charles Scribner's Sons, New York, 1969.

INDEX

Page numbers shown in italics indicate pages on which photographs appear

Accipter, 53
Auk, Great (*Alcidae*), 83, 89; Razor-bill, 89

Bat, 26; Big Brown (*Eptesicus*), 28; Eastern Pipistrelle (*Pipistrellus*), 28; Hoary, 28; Indiana Myotis, 28; Keen's Myotis, 28; Little Brown, *28*; Red (*Lasiurus*), 28; Silver-haired (*Lasionycteris*), 28; Small-footed Myotis, 28; Vampire, 28
Bear, Black, 1, *2*, 28, *29*
Beaver, 3, *8*
Bittern (*Ardeidae*), 75, 76; Least, 76
Blackbird, 63; Bronzed Crow, 63; Red-winged, 63
Bluebird, Eastern, 59
Bobcat, 1, 4, 18, *20*, 21
Bobolink, 63
Bufonidae, 94
Bunting, Snow, 61, 62
Buteos, 53

Cardinal, Northern, 46, 61
Caribou, Woodland, (*Rangifer*) 1, 3, 5, 12, *15*, *16*
Cats, Wild, *Felidae*, 18
Cetacean. *See* Whale
Chickadee, 56, 58
Chipmunk, Eastern, 4, 5, *7*, 8
Coot (*Rallidae*), 73, 75 ; American, *75*
Cormorant, 45, 73, 86; Double-crested, 89; Great, 89
Cottontail, Eastern, (*Sylvilagus*), 11
Cougar, Eastern, 3, 18, *22*
Cowbird, 63
Coyote, *iv*, 16, *19*
Creeper, Brown, 58
Crossbill, Red 61; White-winged, 61
Crow, Common, 56
Cuckoo, Black-billed, 65; Yellow-billed, 65
Curlew, Eskimo, 71

Deer, White-tailed, (*Odocoileus*) *i*, 4, 5, *12*, *13*, 15
Dog, (*Canidae*), 16
Dolphin, 34, 39, 40
Dove, Mourning, 68; Old World Rock, 65
Dovekie, 89
Dowitcher, Short-billed, 69
Duck, American Black, 81; dabbler or puddle, 73, 81, 83; diver, 73, 81, 83; Harlequin, 81; Labrador, 46, 83; Mallard, 78, *79* ; Northern Pintail, 81; Redhead, 83; Ring-necked, 81; Ruddy, 83; Wood, *80*, 81

Eagle, Bald, *iv*, v, 45, 53, *54*; Golden, 53
Egret, 76
Efts, Red, 93
Eider, Common, 83; King, 85
Ermine. *See* Weasel

Falcon, 45; American Kestrel, 53; Merlin, 53; Peregrine, 48, *52*, 53,
Finch, 45, 61; Common Redpole, 61; Purple, 61
Fisher, 3, 21, 22, *24*,
Flicker, Northern, 65
Flycatcher, Olive-sided, 63; Yellow-bellied, 63
Fox, Gray, 5; Red, 16, *18*
Fringillidae, 46, 61
Frog (*Anura*), 91, 94; Bullfrog, 94, *95*, 96, 98; Green, 96, 98; Mink, 96, 98; Northern Leopard, *96*, 98; Northern Spring Peeper, 93; Pickerel, 96; Wood, 96, *97*, 98
Fulmar, Northern, 86

Gadwall, 81
Gannet, Northern, 73, 86, *87*
Goldfinch, American, 61
Goose, 73; Brant, 81; Canada, 73, *78*, 81; Snow, 81
Goshawk, 48
Gossard. *See* Merganser
Grackle, Common, 63
Grebe, 73; Pied-billed, *74*, 75

Grosbeaks, 61; Evening, 61; Pine, 61, *63 ;* Rose-breasted, 61

Groundhog, 5, 12

Grouse, 45, 46; Ruffed, *46;* Spruce, 46, *47,* 48

Guillemot, Black, 89

Gull, 45, 83; Bonaparte's, 86; Great Black-backed, 86; Herring, 83, *84,* 85, 86; Ring-billed, 86

Hare, Arctic, 5, 11; European, (*Lepus capensis*), 11; Snowshoe, 4, 5, 8, *10,* 11

Hawk, 45; Broad-winged, 53; Cooper's, 53; Marsh *51,* 53; Northern Goshawk, 53; Northern Harrier. *See* Marsh; Red-shouldered, 53; Red-tailed, 53; Rough-legged, 53; Sharp-shinned, 53

Heron, 45, 73; Great Blue, 76, *77;* Green, *76 ;* Night. *See* Night-Heron

Hummingbird,Ruby-throated, 45, 46, 66, *67,* 68

Hylidae, 94

Ibis, Glossy, 76

Icteridae, 46, 63

Jaeger, 85

Jay, Blue, 56, *57;* Gray 56

Junco, 62

Killdeer, *71*

Kingbird, 63

Kingfisher, 45; Belted, *65*

Kittiwake, Common, 86

Lion, Mountain, 18

Loon, Common, *72,* 73; Red-throated, 75

Lynx, 4, *21*

Marten, Pine, 3, 21, 22, *25*

Martin, Purple, 63

Meadowlark, Eastern, 63

Merganser, Common, 83; Common Goldeneye, *83;* Hooded, 83; Red-breasted, *82,* 83

Mink, 4, 21, 22, *23,* Giant Sea, 3

Mole, 26, *27;* Eastern Common (*Scalopus*), 26; Hairy-tailed (*Parascalops*), 26; Star-nosed

(*Condylura*), 26

Moose, (*Alces*) 1, 4, 5, *14,* 15

Mouse, Deer, *5;* House, 5; White-footed, 5; Jumping, 5

Mud siren, 91

Mudpuppy, 91

Murre, Common, 89; Thick-billed, 89

Muskrat, 4, 5, 8, *9*

Mustelidae, 21

Newt, *90,* 91, 93; Red-spotted, 93

Night-Heron, Black-crowned, 76

Nighthawk, Common, 68

Nuthatch, 56; Red-breasted, *58*

Opossum (*Marsupialia*), 31; Virginia, 5, *33*

Oriole, Northern 63

Osprey, 45, 53, *55*

Otter, 21, *23*

Owl, 45; Barred, 48, *50,* 51; Boreal, 53; Great Gray, 53; Great Horned, 48; Hawk, 48; Long-eared, 48; Short-eared, 48, *51;* Snowy, 53

Partridge, Hungarian, 48

Parulidae, 46, 59

Passeriformes, 56

Penguin, North Atlantic, 45, 83

Petrel, 83; Leach's, 89

Phalaropes, 69, 70

Pheasant, Ring-neck, 48, *49*

Phoebe, 63

Pigeon, Passenger, 46, 65

Plover, 69; Black-bellied, 71; Lesser Golden, 71; Piping, 71; Upland, 71

Polecat (*fitchet*), 21

Porcupine, *vi,* 1, 4, 11

Porpoise, 39, 40

Ptarmigan, 45, 46; Rock, 48 Willow, 48

Puffin, Atlantic, *88,* 89

Rabbit, Cottontail, 5

Raccoon, 28, *30,* 31

Rail (*Rallidae*), 73, 75 ; King, 75; Virginia, 75; Yellow, 75

Ranidae, 94

Raven, 56

Robin, American, 56, 58, *59*

Sable. *See* Marten

Salamander (*Caudata*), 91; Blue-spotted, 93; Four-toed, 93; Lungless, 93; Mole, 93; Northern Dusky, 93; Northern Two-lined, 93; Redback, 93; Spotted, 93; Yellow-spotted, *92,* 93

Sandpiper (*Scolopacidae*), *44,* 45, 69; Greater Yellowlegs, 69; Least, 69; Lesser Yellowlegs, 69, *70,* 71; Purple, 69; Semipalmated, 69, 71; Solitary, 69; Spotted, 69

Sapsucker, Yellow-bellied, 65

Scaup, Greater, 83; Lesser, 83

Seal, 1, 3; Bay. *See* Harbour; Gray, 34, *35,* 36; Harbour, *36;* Harp, 36, *37,* 39; Hood, 36, 39; Leopard. *See* Harbour; Ranger. *See* Harbour

Shag, 86

Shearwater, 86

Shelduck. *See* Merganser

Shoveller, Northern, 81

Shrew, 4, *26*

Shrike, 53

Skink, Five-lined, 98

Skua, 85

Skunk, Striped, 3, 21, 31, *32*

Snake, 91; Black Rat, 104 ; Eastern Hognosed, 104; Eastern Milk, 104; Eastern Smooth Green, 103, 104; Garter, 100, *101,* 103, 104; Northern Black Racer, 104; Northern Red-bellied, *iv, v, 102.* 103; Northern Ribbon, 103, 104; Northern Ring-necked, 103, 104; Northern Water, 104; Timber Rattlesnake, 98

Snipe, Common, 69

Sora (*Rallidae*), 73, 75

Sparrow, 61; Chipping, 62; Fox, 62; House, 63; Ipswich, 62; Savannah, 62; Song, 62; Swamp, 62; White-crowned, 62; White-throated, 58, 62

Squirrel, Gray, *6,* 7; Red, 4 ; Fox, *7;* Southern Flying, 5

Starling, Common, 63

Swallow, 45; Bank, 63; Barn, 63; Rough-winged, 63; Tree, 63

Swan, Mute, 81

Swift, Chimney, 68

Tadpole, *91*

Teal, Blue-winged, 81; Teal, Green-winged, 81

Tern, 83; Arctic, 86; Common, *85,* 86; Roseate, 83; Hermit, 58. 59; Swainson's, 59; Veery, 59

Toad, 91; Eastern American, *94,* 96; Eastern Spadefoot, 96;, Fowler's, 96; Hudson's Bay, 96

Treefrog, Gray, 96

Turkey, Wild, 48

Turtles, 91, 98, 99, 100; Common Snapping, *98;* Eastern Painted, *99;* Red-Bellied, *100*

Vole, Meadow, 5

Vulture, Turkey, 53

Walrus, 1

Warblers, 58, 61, 62; Chestnut-sided, *62 ;* Common Yellowthroat, *61;* Yellow, *60*

Waxwing, Cedar, 63, 64, 65

Weasel, 21; Common, 22, *25;* Least, 22; Long-tailed, 22; Short-tailed, 22

Whale, (*Delphinidae*) *iv,* 1, 34; Baleen, 34, 39, 40; Beluga, 39; Blue, 39, 43; Fin, 40, 43; Humpback, 40, *41, 42,* 43; Minke, 40, 43; Narwhal, 39; Orca *38,* 39, 40, 43; Pigmy Sperm, 39, 40; Pilot, 39, 40; Right, 40, 42; Sperm, 39, 40, 43; Toothed, 34, 39

Whimbrel, Willet, 69

Widgeon, American, 81

Wolf, Gray, 3, *17*

Wolverine, 3

Wood-Pewee, Eastern 63

Woodchuck. See Groundhog

Woodcock, 69

Woodpecker (*Piciformes*), 65; Downy, 65, *66 ;* Hairy, 65; Pileated, 46, 65; Red-bellied, 65; Red-headed, 65

Wren, House, 58; Marsh, 58; Winter, 58